FLASH

in easy steps

NICK VANDOME

COMPUTER
STEP

in easy steps is an imprint of Computer Step
Southfield Road . Southam . Warwickshire CV47 OFB . England
Tel: +44 (0)1926 817999   Fax: +44 (0)01926 817005

www.ineasysteps.com

Notice of Liability

Every effort has been made to ensure that this book contains accurate and current information. However, Computer Step and the author shall not be liable for any loss or damage suffered by readers as a result of any information contained herein.

Trademarks

Flash™ is a trademark of Macromedia, Inc. All other trademarks are acknowledged as belonging to their respective companies.

Printed and bound in the United Kingdom

ISBN 1-84078-106-8

Contents

1   Introducing Flash   7

Life before Flash	8
How Flash works	9
The uses for Flash	11
What Flash can do	12
Animation	12
Interactivity	13
Obtaining Flash	14
The Flash Player	15
Installing Flash	16
The Flash environment	17
Flash movies	18

2   Getting started   19

Basic functions	20
The Timeline	22
The Stage	23
The Toolbars	28
The Menu bar	30
The Inspectors	33
Object	33
Frame	33
Transform	34
Scene	34
Generator	34
Viewing options	35
Preferences	36

3   Creating objects   37

Drawing in Flash	38
The Drawing toolbar	42
Line tool	43
Oval tool	44
Rectangle tool	46
Pencil tool	47
Brush tool	50
Ink Bottle tool	51
Paint Bucket tool	52
Dropper tool	53

Eraser tool 54
Hand and Magnifier tools 56
Arrow tool 57
Lasso tool 58

Editing objects 59

4

Selecting with the Arrow tool 60
Selecting with the Lasso tool 63
Editing lines 64
Grouping objects 65
Moving objects 66
Resizing objects 67
Rotating and skewing objects 69
Rapid rotation and flipping 71
Reshaping objects 72
Copy and Paste 74
Aligning objects 75
Stacking order 77
Cut-aways 78

Colour and text 79

5

Standard Colour palette 80
Adding solid colours 81
Adding gradients 83
Editing gradient fills 85
Colour focus 87
Selecting colours 88
Adding text 89
To add a text label 89
To add a text box 90
Formatting text 91
Manipulating text 92

Symbols and instances 93

6

Symbols and instances defined 94
The Library 96
Creating symbols – the conversion route 100
Creating a new symbol 102
Symbol Editing Mode 104
Editing symbols 105
Duplicating symbols 106
Editing instances 107

7 — Bitmaps and sound — 109

Using bitmaps — 110
Importing bitmaps — 111
Bitmap properties — 112
Tracing bitmaps — 113
Bitmaps as fills — 114
Using sound — 117
Importing sounds — 118
Editing sounds — 119

8 — Frames and layers — 121

Working with frames — 122
   Keyframes — 122
   Regular frames — 124
Adding frames — 125
Deleting and copying frames — 127
Frame properties — 128
About layers — 129
Working with layers — 130
Inserting layers — 131
Deleting and copying layers — 132
Layer modes — 133
Layer properties — 134
Mask layers — 135

9 — Animation — 137

Animation basics — 138
Elements of animation — 139
   The Timeline — 139
   Timeline status bar — 139
   The Playhead — 140
   Onion skinning — 140
Scenes — 142
   Adding a new scene — 142
   Renaming a scene — 143
Frame-by-frame animation — 144
Motion tweening — 147
Motion guides — 150
Motion guide orientation — 151
Shape tweening — 152
Animating text — 155
Movie clips — 156

Interactivity   157

10

Types of interactivity   158
Frame actions   159
   Adding frame actions   159
   Types of actions   160
   Deleting actions   161
Adding Stop and Play actions   162
Adding Go To actions   163
Inserting a preloader   165
Button symbols   167
Adding actions to buttons   170
Adding movie clips and sounds   172

Testing and publishing   173

11

Testing options   174
   The Controller   174
   Enable buttons and frames   174
   Testing scenes   175
   Testing movies   175
Testing environment   176
Preparing to publish   180
   Publish settings for the Web   180
   HTML settings   181
   Flash settings   183
More publishing options   184
Publishing a movie   185
Publishing on the Web   186

Index   187

Introducing Flash

This chapter gives an overview of the functions of Flash and the uses to which it can be put. It shows how to obtain and install the program and gives details of the Flash environment when it is first opened.

Covers

Life before Flash | 8

How Flash works | 9

The uses for Flash | 11

What Flash can do | 12

Obtaining Flash | 14

The Flash Player | 15

Installing Flash | 16

The Flash environment | 17

Flash movies | 18

Chapter One

Life before Flash

Bandwidth is a term used to describe the amount of digital data that can be sent down a telephone cable and the speed at which it is sent. A higher bandwidth means that more information can be sent down a cable, and so reach the user's computer more quickly. Since multimedia files can be a lot larger than their static counterparts, increased bandwidth is vital for them to download quickly enough to keep the user's attention.

Increased bandwidth for the Internet is an area that telecommunications companies are constantly working on improving.

If there is one constant about the Internet and the World Wide Web it is the speed at which they develop. As recently as the beginning of the 1990s Web users were excited about the possibility of viewing coloured static text and a few small, equally static, images. However, since then Web site designers and developers have harnessed advances in technology with a desire to create increasingly complicated multimedia output. This includes animated images, animated text, page transitions, sound and video.

Initially even the most basic multimedia effects on the Web came at a price: downloading time. In a lot of cases the infrastructure for downloading multimedia pages was just not up to the task, with the result that these types of pages took a long time to appear on the user's computer. The result of this was a lot of annoyed users and a lot of sites that were left unvisited because they took too long to download.

But as with everything on the Web, the technology has not been slow to catch up and, due to increased bandwidth for downloading and more advanced browsers for viewing, it is now possible to enjoy truly exceptional multimedia experiences on the Web, without having to wait an eternity for the files to download.

In addition to increased bandwidth, software programs for creating multimedia sites have become increasingly powerful and this is where Flash comes in. Flash is an animation program that can produce high quality multimedia files. In addition to this it uses a number of techniques to ensure that the final product is as streamlined as possible, thus creating files that can be downloaded reasonably quickly. Three of the most important aspects of Flash in this respect are:

- Vector-based graphics

- Streaming

- Compression

How Flash works

Vector-based graphics

Traditionally, images on the Web have been bitmaps i.e. images that are made up of pixels, or tiny coloured dots. In general, the more pixels in an image then the better the quality. However, each pixel adds to the file size of the image and so you have to walk a fine line between quality and file size. Also, when a bitmap image is resized it can deteriorate in quality: if it is enlarged, then each individual pixel has to cover a larger area. This can result in the edges looking jaggy or ragged. The three types of bitmap images that are used on the Web are GIFs (Graphical Interchange Format), JPEGs (Joint Photographic Experts Group) and PNGs (Portable Network Group).

GIFs are created with 256 colours so they are generally used for graphics that do not have an enormous range of colour depth. JPEGs use 16 million colours and are more commonly used for photographic images. PNGs are not yet as popular as GIFs or JPEGs but they can produce good quality images with small file sizes.

Since one of the main functions of Flash is creating drawing objects, it is vital that it can do this in an efficient and high quality way. It achieves this by using a vector-based system for producing graphics, rather than a pixel-based one. A vector-based system is one where objects, lines and fills are created using mathematical equations. The computer then interprets this equation and displays the corresponding image on the screen. This has two considerable advantages:

- Since vector-based images do not consist of any actual pixels, they are usually a lot smaller in file size than their bitmap counterparts. Even very complicated vector-based images create comparatively small files, regardless of how large or small a size they are displayed at

Drawing programs (such as Macromedia Freehand and Adobe Illustrator) use vector-based systems for creating graphics.

- Vector-based images lose very little image quality when they are resized, since they are still based on the same mathematical equation. So, if a bitmap circle is increased in size, its edges may begin to look ragged. However, a vector-based circle would appear smooth regardless of how it was resized. This combination of small file size and high quality makes vector-based graphics ideal for Web pages

A Flash file is known as a movie.

Streaming is a bit like reading a book by having each page handed to you as you need it: you know it is all there, but you can only read one part at a time so seeing the whole thing at once would be pointless.

Streaming

The end product created by Flash (called a Flash movie) can be either a few seconds long or several minutes. With the former, downloading time is not a big issue because the browser should be able to download all of the movie and play it almost simultaneously. However, with the latter the situation is not so straightforward. Even with all of the tricks it has up its sleeve, Flash would be hard pushed to produced a movie that would play for several minutes and yet be compact enough to download in a few seconds.

Flash overcomes this problem with a technique called streaming. This feeds information to the browser as it needs it to play the movie, without having to wait for the whole thing to be downloaded to get started. So initially Flash will feed enough of the movie for the browser to start playing it and the user will see this on their monitor. As the movie begins to play, Flash continues to feed information to the browser, enabling it to play the next part of the movie. This is streaming in action and it means that even the longest Flash movie can be viewed without having to wait hours for it to begin after downloading.

Another important way in which Flash controls the overall file size of a movie is through the use of Symbols and Instances. This allows for copies of an original image to be used numerous times without adding to the size of the movie. This is covered in greater detail in Chapter Six.

Compression

Most images on the Web are compressed in one way or another. GIFs, JPEGs and PNGs all use various forms of compression to decrease their file size. In the majority of cases this has, at worst, only a minimal effect on the final image. One reason for this is that computer monitors can only display between 72–96 pixels per inch. This is known as the resolution and if an image has a higher resolution than this then it is creating an unnecessarily large file, with extra pixels that cannot be displayed.

Flash uses a variety of sophisticated compression techniques, for both images and sounds. The technical side of this is best left to the experts but there are some preference settings that can be used to determine various compression settings. These will be looked at in the relevant chapters.

The uses for Flash

Web authoring

Although Flash movies can be output through a variety of devices, their main function is in the production of Web pages. However, there is one important point that should be remembered in relation to this: Flash movies have to be incorporated into HTML documents to enable them to be displayed on the Web. This means you have to create the HTML pages for your site and then insert the relevant Flash movies. Luckily, Flash has a facility for producing HTML files that incorporate Flash movies and this is looked at in Chapter Eleven. The end result looks complicated, but Flash takes care of most of this behind the scenes.

If you are creating Web pages that include Flash movies it is important to include a plain HTML version of the document. This is because not all users will be able to, or want to, download the Flash Player that is needed to view Flash movies. So on the home page of a Web site there could be three links:

- *to the Flash version of the site*
- *to the HTML version, and;*
- *for downloading the Player*

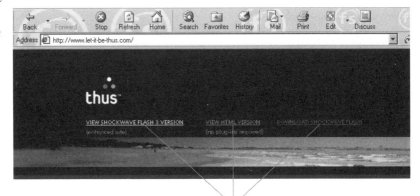

Web pages containing Flash movies should also have a plain HTML alternative, and links for downloading the Flash Player

Presentations

In addition to be being used on Web pages, Flash movies can also be used as a presentation tool. To do this, the Flash movie is played through a computer as a stand- alone application. This is known as creating a projector and this is a self-contained executable program that can play a movie regardless of whether the user has the Flash Player installed or not.

Flash movies can also be exported into video formats such as QuickTime or a Windows .AVI movie.

What Flash can do

Animation

It is perfectly possible to produce Flash movies that contain nothing more than static text and images. However, if this is your aim you would be well advised to use an HTML program such as FrontPage or PageMill if you are creating Web pages and PowerPoint if you are creating presentations. One of Flash's main reasons for existing is its ability to animate both text and graphics. If you do not use this then you are overlooking at least 50% of the program's capabilities.

While Flash may not turn you into the next Walt Disney it does offer a considerable range of techniques for the budding animator:

- Text that fades in and out or moves across the screen

- Frame-by-frame animation, using either objects you have drawn yourself or items you import into Flash

- Tweened animation, a technique where you set the start and end point for an object and Flash automatically creates an animation between (hence the name) the two points. Tweened animations can be in the form of either motion or shape tweens

1 ₹ 2

- Guided animation, where you create a path which the animated object can follow

Interactivity

Another key element of Flash is interactivity. This allows the user not only to view a Flash movie but also to interact with it. This makes users feel as if they are actually part of the movie they are viewing and that their actions affect what is happening on screen.

Interactivity in Flash is created by assigning certain values and properties to buttons and text boxes so that one action triggers another, predefined one. This opens up numerous possibilities for Flash movies:

Creating interactive elements in a Flash movie is one of the more complex areas of the program. It is important to feel comfortable with the rest of the program before you begin using interactive functions. See Chapter Ten for more information on interactivity.

- Buttons can have action commands assigned to them, to define what acts as a trigger. This can be when a button is pressed, when it is released, or when the mouse cursor passes over it

- Buttons can have actions that play sounds at certain points in the movie

- Buttons can be programmed to jump automatically to another part of the same movie

- Buttons can be programmed to open up other pages on the Web

- Buttons can be used to create a Menu bar

- Text boxes can be used to display a personalised message to the user when they insert an item of text, such as their name

- Text boxes can be used to collect information about the user. This is done with an interactive form and the data is then collected by the server that is hosting the page with the Flash movie on it (if the Flash movie is on a Web page)

Obtaining Flash

There is virtually no difference between the PC format of Flash or the Mac one. Most of the screen views and menus are identical. Any differences will be noted as and when they occur.

Flash is produced by Macromedia and detailed information about the program can be found on their Web site at:

- http://www.macromedia.com/software/flash

This contains general information about the program, demos of how it works and links to sites that use Flash.

Click here: to download a 30-day trial version of the program. This is a fully functioning version of the program that will stop working at the end of the trial period.

The Flash home page on the Macromedia site

Click here on the trial version to buy the full program. You will be taken through the online purchase process step-by-step

In addition to downloading Flash, you can also buy the program from computer shops and software retailers. The price is approximately £240 and this includes disks for the PC and the Mac formats.

When the trial version has been downloaded, click here to try it

The Flash Player

In order to view a Flash movie on the Web, the Flash Player has to be installed on the user's computer. This is a plug-in application that allows the user to see the Flash movie playing. The Player is installed automatically when you install the full authoring program of Flash. However, if you want to view Flash-enabled Web pages before you buy the program then you will have to download the Player. This can be done from the Flash Home Page:

1 Select download> Flash Player 4

2 Follow the steps for downloading the Player

Installing Flash

Playback via the Flash Player requires the following features:

• *Windows 3.1 or later or NT 3.5.1 or later. (Mac OS 7.1 or later for Macintosh users)*

• *Internet Explorer 3 or later*

• *Netscape Navigator 2 or later, or;*

• *A Java-enabled browser if you are using the Java Edition of the Player*

If you are using an older version of a browser the easiest option is to upgrade to the latest version. These are free and can be found at:

• *http://www.microsoft. com for Internet Explorer, and;*

• *http://www.netscape.com for Netscape Navigator/ Communicator*

If you are installing Flash by downloading it from the Macromedia Web site, or from a CD-ROM, the process is similar. When the program begins to run, the Flash 4 Installer icon will appear. Double-click on this to go to the Flash introduction window. Click OK and then follow the step-by-step instructions that take you through the installation process. Flash will set up folders on your hard drive for the program and, unless you have a good reason not to, it is best to install the program files here.

System requirements

The system requirements for Flash have to take into consideration the authoring program and also the Flash Player for viewing the end results (see the tip).

Windows authoring

• 133 MHz Pentium processor

• Windows 95/98, NT4 or later

• 32 Mb of RAM

• 20 Mb of disk space (ROM)

• 256-colour monitor with minimum 800 x 600 resolution

• CD-ROM drive

Mac authoring

• Power Mac or iMac with OS 7.5 or later

• 32 Mb of RAM

• 20 Mb of available disk space (ROM)

• 256-colour monitor with minimum 800 x 600 resolution

• CD-ROM drive

The Flash environment

For users of previous versions of Flash, the following areas have been enhanced in Flash 4:

- *Timeline*
- *Layers*
- *Toolbar*
- *Library*
- *Inspectors*
- *Animation, and;*
- *Publishing*

There are two other important Flash authoring components that do not appear initially. These are the Library and the Inspectors. Both of these are accessed through Window on the Menu bar.

The elements of the Flash authoring environment are looked at in greater detail in Chapter Two.

Once Flash has been installed, it can be opened by double-clicking the Flash icon that the installation process should have placed on the Desktop (Windows) or in the Finder (Mac):

Double-click this icon to launch Flash

The first view

When Flash is first opened, a new, blank document will be displayed on screen. This is the Flash authoring environment and it contains the elements that are needed to create a Flash movie. At first sight, it can seen a bit overwhelming, but each item has an important part to play in the authoring process:

The Menu bar   The Standard Toolbar (Windows only)

The Layers section (where different layers are added to a movie)

The Drawing Toolbar (holds the drawing tools)

The Stage (the content for each movie is placed here)

The Timeline (specifies how the movie is played and various actions that occur)

Flash movies

Movie files

When Flash files are created and displayed they are known as movies. However, two separate sets of files are used to create the movies and then play them. When the movie is created in the authoring environment this results in Flash-format files that have the extension: .FLA. When the file is transferred to be played on the Flash Player it is in the playable format, which has the extension: .SWF, which stands for Shockwave Flash. So each Flash movie has a minimum of at least two sets of files:

When Flash movies are published in Web documents another file format is also created – HTML. However, the Flash publishing function makes this process a lot more painless than it may at first seem (see Chapter Eleven).

Flash authoring files:

Flash movie files:

Frames

Even if a movie consisted of only one frame, it would still be possible to create an animation. This could be done by using a movie clip and inserting it in the frame. Movie clips are looked at in more detail in Chapter Nine.

Just as with hand-drawn animations, Flash movies are made up of a series of frames that are played in sequence. It is possible to create animated effects by placing slightly different versions of an image in adjacent frames and then playing them from the beginning. However, it is also possible to add a wide variety of content to each frame: backgrounds, text, sounds and interactive buttons. A Flash movie can consist of a single frame or it can have several hundred.

Frames are identified by the grid of boxes along the Timeline.

Getting started

This chapter looks at the elements that make up the Flash authoring environment. This includes the means for controlling the content of a movie, the area where movies are created, and the toolbars and menus that are used during the editing process.

Covers

Basic functions | 20

The Timeline | 22

The Stage | 23

The Toolbars | 28

The Menu bar | 30

The Inspectors | 33

Viewing options | 35

Preferences | 36

Chapter Two

Basic functions

In Windows only, new movies can be created and existing ones opened by using the two icons on the left of the Standard toolbar:

New files

Open files

If you want to edit an existing Flash file, make sure you open the authoring format file rather than the movie-format one. If you open the movie one it will display the movie as it will appear when it is published and you will not be able to edit it. Authoring files have a .FLA file extension and movie files have a .SWF extension.

Opening and closing files

Flash movies are created in the Flash Editor section of the program and this is the environment that appears when Flash is launched. The Editor opens with a new, empty document called Movie1. All new movies that are created in the same editing session are called Movie... and numbered sequentially, until they are saved and given a unique name. To create a new Flash movie:

1 Select File>New from the Menu bar

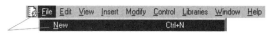

2 The new movie is opened and its current name is displayed here

To open an existing Flash movie:

1 Select File>Open from the Menu bar

2 Click on the file you want to open and select Open

Flash windows

Windows in the Flash environment adopt the standards operated by both Windows and Macintosh on their respective platforms. Window controls can help specify how Flash files are displayed while you are editing them.

Windows controls

The Close button for an active movie, closes that particular movie. The Close button for Flash (the one always at the top of the screen), closes the program.

Minimise window — Restore window — Maximise window — Close window — Scroll bars — Scroll arrows — Resize button. Click and drag to resize

Macintosh controls

Close window — Zoom to fit — Collapse window — Scrollbars — Scroll arrows — Resize button. Click and drag to resize

The Timeline

The Timeline is the section of Flash that enables you to organise all of the elements that make up your movie and see what is placed at certain points throughout your publication. The Timeline organises items such as scenes, layers and frames and it is also used to create animated effects. Of all of the elements of Flash, the Timeline is probably the most important and also the most complicated for the novice as there is no equivalent in other software packages.

The Timeline contains several powerful organisational functions

Click and drag here to reposition the Timeline

Click and drag here to resize the Timeline

Elements of the Timeline

Current scene   Layer controls   Playhead   Frames   Movie scenes   Movie symbols

Layers

Frame rate

Insert layer or motion guide   Delete layer   Playhead options   Onion skinning   Current frame

The Stage

The Library is an area for storing reusable items in a movie. This is looked at in greater detail in Chapter Six.

The Stage is the area where all of the content for a Flash movie is placed. This can be done by drawing objects directly onto the Stage, dragging them from the Flash Library or importing them from other applications. At any given frame in a Flash movie, the contents for that frame are displayed on the Stage. So the contents for frame 1 could look very different from the contents of frame 20 in a movie. The grey area around the Stage is known as the Work Area and this can be used to place animated objects that appear or disappear from the edge of the Stage. Only items that are visible within the Stage area will appear in the final movie.

The Flash Stage can be thought of in the same way as a theatre stage: anything that is placed there can be viewed by the audience.

Click and drag the Playhead to move between the frames of a movie. The content for each frame that is covered by the Playhead will be displayed on the Stage

To hide the Work Area, select View from the Menu bar and deselect the tick next to Work Area. To display it again, reverse the process.

The Stage, displaying the content for the current frame (in this case frame 1)

The Work Area. Items placed here will not appear in the final movie but it can be a starting or ending point for items that move on or off the Stage

Movie Properties dialog box

There are a number of settings that can be applied to the Stage and these are accessed through the Movie Properties dialog box:

1 Select Modify>Movie from the Menu bar

2 Various settings can be applied through the Movie Properties dialog box:

The default frame rate may not be the actual rate at which a movie is played on the user's browser. This is because they may have an older browser or a slower modem, so they cannot download the frames quickly enough. It could also be caused by certain parts of a movie being very processor intensive.

This problem can be partly overcome by testing the movie before it is published and this is looked at in Chapter Eleven.

Frame rate

Stage dimensions

Grid spacing

Grid colour

Save new default

Ruler settings

Background colour

Show/ Hide grid

The settings in the Movie Properties dialog box affect a Flash movie as follows:

• *Frame Rate.* This is the speed, in frames per second, at which the movie is set to play. The default setting is 12 frames per second and this is regarded as a reliable standard setting for animations viewed on the Web

To set the Stage size to exactly fit the content in a specific movie, select Match>Contents from the Movie Properties dialog box. Flash will then automatically calculate the dimensions required for the Stage.

- *Stage Dimensions*. This specifies the size at which the Stage is displayed. Type values into the Dimensions boxes to make the Stage larger or smaller as required

- *Ruler settings*. This specifies the unit of measurement for all affected items on the Stage: rulers, grids and Stage dimensions. The choices are: inches, decimal inches, points, centimetres, millimetres and pixels

- *Grid settings*. This specifies the settings for the Stage grid (see overleaf)

- *Background*. For these settings, see below

Setting the background colour

The default background colour on the Stage is white, but it can be changed as required. The background colour will appear in any part of the finished movie that is not covered by other objects on the Stage. To set the background colour for a movie:

The Stage colour will act as the default background for the whole of a movie. If the colour is changed at any point in the movie this will be reflected in the rest of the file too.

1   Select Background from the Movie Properties dialog box

2   Select a colour from the Colour palette. This will be the new background colour for the whole of the Stage

The Stage grid

It is possible to superimpose a grid over the Stage, to enable exact positioning and sizing of objects that are placed there. The grid is only visible in the authoring environment and it does not appear in the final, published movie. To display the grid:

Make sure there is a good contrast between the colour of the grid and the Stage background. Otherwise the grid will not be clearly visible, which rather defeats the purpose of having it there.

1 Select Show Grid in the Movie Properties dialog so that a tick is showing

For the grid to be at its most effective, the Snap option has to be turned on. This means that items aligned with the grid will automatically 'snap' to the nearest grid line, for precise alignment.

To activate this, select View>Snap, so that a tick appears next to Snap. If you want to position items independently of the grid, turn the Snap option off by deselecting the tick.

2 Select a colour for the grid by clicking here and selecting a colour from the palette that appears

3 Select the spacing for the grid lines by entering it here. The measurement value is the same as in the Ruler Units box (see the facing page)

4 The grid appears over the entire Stage

Adding rulers

To further increase the precision for placing objects within a movie, rulers can be added to the Stage so that items can be positioned exactly where they are required. To add rulers to a movie:

When you first start using Flash you may not feel the need to use the rulers very often. But as you use the program more and begin to create more complex movies you may find the rulers invaluable for placing, moving and resizing items when you have numerous objects on the Stage at once. In some cases the rulers may be activated for the entire authoring process.

1 Select View>Rulers so a tick appears

2 The rulers appear along the top and the left-hand side of the Stage (in this example the measurement used for the rulers is pixels)

3 If a new measurement value is entered in the Ruler Unit box in the Movie Properties dialog box, this will then serve as the default for the ruler on the Stage

The Toolbars

The Flash toolbars are collections of buttons that offer quick access to several of the editing and drawing functions within the program. The toolbars differ slightly between the Windows and the Mac versions of Flash:

Mac toolbars

The tools in the Drawing toolbar are looked at in more detail in Chapter Three.

The Mac toolbars consist of only the Drawing toolbar and the Controller toolbar. The Drawing toolbar contains all of the tools required to draw objects in Flash and the Controller toolbar is used to play through a movie while it is being edited in the authoring environment.

The Mac toolbars are accessed by selecting Window>Toolbar (for the Drawing toolbar) or Window>Controller

The Standard toolbar has icons that act as shortcuts for commonly used items on the Menu bar, such as Open, New, Save and Print. The Status bar denotes whether Caps Lock and Num Lock are on.

Windows toolbars

In addition to the Drawing and the Controller toolbars, the Windows version of Flash also has a Standard toolbar and a Status bar. These are accessed by selecting View from the Menu bar and then checking on the appropriate option.

The Standard toolbar

The Status bar

Tips can be activated for the toolbars, so that when the cursor is placed over an icon a small pop-up line of text appears, explaining what that item does. On the Mac, select File> Preferences and check on the Show Tooltips box. In Windows, select Options>Show Tooltips from the Menu bar.

Moving the toolbars

Although the toolbars appear in their default positions when Flash is first opened, it is possible to move them around the screen, depending on your own preferences and your editing needs for particular items in a movie. The behaviour of the Mac and the Windows Flash toolbars is slightly different:

Moving Mac toolbars

With the Mac version of Flash, the Drawing and Controller toolbars can be moved around the screen. If you keep moving them, parts of them may disappear from view:

1 Click here and drag to move the toolbar

2 If the toolbar is moved too far, parts of it may disappear

If a toolbar is docked along the top or bottom of the screen, it appears as a horizontal line of icons. If it is docked to the left or right of the screen it appears as a vertical line.

Moving Windows toolbars

The Standard, Drawing and Controller toolbars can all be moved in the Windows version of Flash. In addition they can also be docked to the perimeter of the screen:

1 Click and hold anywhere where there is no icon. Drag the toolbar to a new location

2 The toolbars can be docked along any screen border – they do not disappear off the edge

The Menu bar

The Menu bar provides access to the core elements of Flash for editing movies. This covers all of the functions that are required to create, edit and test a Flash movie.

If a menu item has a right-pointing arrow after it, this means that there is a sub-menu linked to the main item. Click on the arrow to view the sub-menu.

The File menu

This contains menus for basic functions such as opening and saving movies and setting preferences for editing and publishing:

File	
New	⌘N
Open...	⌘O
Open as Library...	Shift ⌘O
Close	⌘W
Save	⌘S
Save As...	Shift ⌘S
Revert	
Import...	⌘R
Export Movie...	Option Shift ⌘S
Export Image...	
Publish Settings...	Shift ⌘F12
Publish Preview	▶
Publish	Shift F12
Page Setup...	
Print Margins...	
Print Preview	
Print...	⌘P
Preferences...	
Assistant...	
1 Flash Guy	
2 Creating a Movie Clip.fla	
3 Fighter	
4 Flash Baby	
Quit	⌘Q

The elements of each menu will be looked at in greater detail as they occur throughout the book.

The Edit menu

This contains commands for editing items within a movie (e.g. Copy and Paste, selection tools and inserting objects):

Edit	
Undo	⌘Z
Redo	⌘Y
Cut	⌘X
Copy	⌘C
Paste	⌘V
Paste in Place	Shift ⌘V
Clear	Delete
Duplicate	⌘D
Select All	⌘A
Deselect All	Shift ⌘A
Copy Frames	Opt ⌘C
Paste Frames	Opt ⌘V
Edit Symbols	⌘E
Edit Selected	
Edit All	

The View menu

This gives you control of how your movie looks on screen. This includes showing and hiding items, viewing the movie at its actual size and smoothing the edges of shapes on the Stage:

View	
Goto	▶
100%	⌘1
Show Frame	⌘2
Show All	⌘3
Outlines	Option Shift ⌘O
Fast	Option Shift ⌘F
✓Antialias	Option Shift ⌘A
Antialias Text	Option Shift ⌘T
✓Timeline	Option ⌘T
✓Work Area	Shift ⌘W
Rulers	Option Shift ⌘R
Grid	Option Shift ⌘G
Snap	Option ⌘G
Show Shape Hints	Option ⌘H

The Insert menu

This allows you to manipulate objects, layers and frames. It also has a function for creating a moving animation – Create Motion Tween:

Insert	
Convert to Symbol...	F8
New Symbol...	⌘F8
Layer	
Motion Guide	
Frame	F5
Delete Frame	Shift F5
Keyframe	F6
Blank Keyframe	F7
Clear Keyframe	Shift F6
Create Motion Tween	
Scene	
Remove Scene	

Menus that only apply to specific items are also available in Flash. These are known as contextual menus and they show the options that are available for a particular item. This can be anything within the Flash window.

These menus can be accessed by moving the cursor over the item whose contextual menu you want to see. Then right-click (Windows) or Ctrl+click (Mac) and the menu connected with that item will appear.

The Modify menu

This is used to access dialog boxes affecting the properties of items such as layers, scenes and the whole movie. It also provides for some general formatting:

Modify	
Instance...	⌘I
Frame...	⌘F
Layer...	
Scene...	
Movie...	⌘M
Font...	⌘T
Paragraph...	Shift ⌘T
Style	▶
Kerning	▶
Text Field...	Option ⌘F
Transform	▶
Arrange	▶
Curves	▶
Frames	▶
Trace Bitmap...	
Align...	⌘K
Group	⌘G
Ungroup	Shift ⌘G
Break Apart	⌘B

The Control menu

This lets you test your movie and see how various parts of it, or the whole thing, will look when it is played back:

Control	
Play	Return
Rewind	Option ⌘R
Step Forward	>
Step Backward	<
Test Movie	⌘Return
Test Scene	Option ⌘Return
Loop Playback	
Play All Scenes	
Enable Frame Actions	Option ⌘A
Enable Buttons	Option ⌘B
Mute Sounds	Option ⌘M

The Library is an area for keeping items that are going to be reused within a Flash movie. Each new movie starts with an empty Library and this is where you will place the reusable objects you create during the movie authoring process.

The Libraries menu provides samples of reusable items, all stored in their own libraries.

The Libraries menu

This shows the samples Flash has stored in the various system libraries. These are buttons, graphics, movie clips and sounds:

Libraries
Buttons
Buttons-Advanced
Graphics
Movie Clips
Sounds

The Window menu

This determines how the open windows are displayed, gives access to the Inspectors and, on the Mac, gives access to the toolbars:

Window	
New Window	Option ⌘N
Arrange All	
Cascade	
✓**Toolbar**	
Inspectors	▶
✓**Controller**	
Colors	
Output	
Generator Objects	
Library	⌘L
✓1 Untitled 1	

If you have not already done so, it is worth working through the Flash lessons. Select Help>Lessons and follow the eight lessons that are available. Each one should not take much more than about fifteen minutes.

The Help menu

This provides online help in the form of Balloon Help and also the Flash help topics, lessons and samples:

Help
About Balloon Help...
Show Balloons
Flash Help Topics
Register Flash
Flash Developers Center
Lessons...
Samples...

The Inspectors

Inspectors are an element of Flash that give additional information about various items that are on the Stage. There are five Inspector windows and they are all accessed by selecting Window>Inspectors and then selecting the relevant Inspector. The five Inspector windows are:

By default, the first four Inspectors are grouped together. To access each Inspector, click on the appropriate tab. To ungroup one of the Inspectors, click and drag one of the tabs. This will separate it from the other Inspectors. Drag back to regroup.

Object

This displays the size of an item on the Stage and its position in regard to the top and left-hand side of the Stage.

The size and position of objects can be changed by altering the relevant values in the boxes of the Object Inspector

Tabs

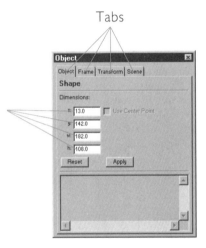

Frame

This Inspector provides information about the active frame i.e. the one that is currently being worked on.

Actions in Flash are commands that tell an item in a movie to perform a certain task. They are involved with interactivity and this is discussed in greater detail in Chapter Ten.

The Frame Inspector contains information about the currently selected frame e.g.:

- its type
- any labels or comments associated with it
- any sounds in the frame
- any assigned actions

Flash can generate copies of objects through its use of symbols and instances. This is a technique whereby numerous copies can be created from one original. However, Flash ensures that the copies are a lot smaller in terms of disk space used. This leads to more streamlined movies and it is an excellent way to copy items in a movie.

Symbols and instances are a vital part of Flash and they are looked at in greater detail in Chapter Six.

Transform

This Inspector can be used to skew and rotate objects, or to show how much a copy of an object (an 'instance') differs from the original.

If a simple object is selected, values can be entered to rotate and skew it. If it is a copy of the original, the default values will show how much it differs from the original. These values can then be altered if required

Scene

This Inspector can be used to organise the scenes in a movie.

The scenes in the movie are listed in the Scene Inspector. Scenes can be added, deleted, copied or can have their properties checked

More information about the Generator Inspector can be found at:

• *http://www.macromedia. com/generator*

(There are no spaces in the address.)

Generator

This Inspector is used to activate the generator option within Flash. This can be used to personalise Web sites.

Viewing options

During the editing process it is important to be able to view the contents of the Stage at different magnifications. On some occasions you will want to zoom in on objects to edit them or position them precisely, while on others you will want to view the entire Stage so you can see how various elements appear in relation to others. This can be done by using either the View pop-up menu or the Magnifier tool.

In Windows, the View pop-up menu is accessed from the Standard toolbar. On the Mac it is accessed from the Drawing toolbar.

View pop-up menu

This allows you to select various magnification levels for viewing the Stage:

Show Frame displays the objects on the Stage and Show All displays the objects on the Stage and the Work Area, at the most appropriate size.

1 Click here

2 Select a viewing option from the pop-up menu

Magnifier tool

This can be used to magnify a certain part of the Stage.

Magnify an object on the Stage by clicking on it once with the Magnification tool. Or click and drag so that a rectangle is drawn around the object. The items inside will be magnified.

1 Click here to select the Magnification tool and choose whether you want to increase or decrease the magnification

Preferences

The Preferences menu can be used to determine certain settings for a movie, either before you start creating it or during the editing process. The Preferences menu can be accessed by selecting File > Preferences and it is slightly different for both Windows and the Mac:

Windows

Settings for how bitmaps are handled when copied onto the Clipboard

The no. of Undo operations that can be performed

PostScript printing, Shift Select and Timeline preferences

Mac

Settings for PICT images (a Mac image file format) saved on the Clipboard

The no. of Undo operations that can be performed

Shift Select option. This determines if you need to hold down Shift to select multiple objects

Show Tooltips and Timeline docking preferences

Creating objects

This chapter looks at the basics of drawing objects in Flash and gives an overview of the contents of the Drawing toolbar.

Covers

Drawing in Flash | 38

The Drawing toolbar | 42

Line tool | 43

Oval tool | 44

Rectangle tool | 46

Pencil tool | 47

Brush tool | 50

Ink Bottle tool | 51

Paint Bucket tool | 52

Dropper tool | 53

Eraser tool | 54

Hand and Magnifier tools | 56

Arrow tool | 57

Lasso tool | 58

Chapter Three

Drawing in Flash

One of the most powerful elements of Flash is its drawing tools. At first sight these may seem as if they are capable of little more than creating a variety of lines and shapes, such as circles and squares. However, these tools are a lot more versatile than this and, with practise and a small degree of artistic flair, they can be used to create an array of stunning graphical images. Before you get started with creating objects with the drawing tools there are a few areas to look at that have a major impact on drawing operations in Flash.

Overlay objects are created by grouping together two or more drawing objects. For instance, if you have created an image of a wall with dozens of rectangles as the bricks, this can be grouped together to make a single item. This is done by selecting Modify>Group from the Menu bar. Once objects have been grouped together they become a single overlay object.

Overlay objects can also be created by converting graphics into 'symbols'. This is discussed in greater detail in Chapter Six.

Stage level and overlay level objects

Simple objects are created in Flash with one of the drawing tools on the Stage. At this point they are in their most basic form and are known as 'stage level objects' i.e. they are placed directly on the Stage. However, it is also possible to convert objects into 'overlay level objects'. This in effect places them on a transparent film just above the Stage. To the naked eye, a stage level object and an overlay level object are identical. However, they both act differently within the Flash environment:

- Stage level objects are more versatile for editing purposes

- Stage level objects always reside on the Stage and they are covered by anything that is placed on top of them

Stage level object — Overlay level object

Within the same layer, overlay level objects will always cover stage level ones

- Stage level objects can interact with each other, i.e. one stage level object can be placed over another similar object and, if the first one is moved, the covered portion of the second object is then cut away:

If you want to convert an overlay level object back to a stage level one, perhaps for editing purposes, this can be done by selecting the object and selecting Modify>Break Apart from the Menu bar.

1 Draw two stage level objects, with parts of them overlapping

2 Select the Arrow tool and click and drag to select part of both objects

Several stage level objects can overlap on the Stage without affecting each other, if they are created on separate layers. Layers are looked at in greater detail in Chapter Eight.

3 Drag away the selected portion. This interaction between shapes can only be done with stage level objects. Since overlay level objects reside on a different level they do not actually 'touch' stage level ones

- Stage level objects are usually used when creating new graphics, while object level ones are used for the final version of the image

Strokes and fills

Solid objects drawn in Flash, such as circles and squares, are created by using an outline and a fill. In Flash terminology, these are known as strokes and fills respectively. Strokes and fills can be specified before a shape is created, or they can be edited at any time during the creation of the movie. Both stage level and overlay level objects can have their strokes and fills edited independently of each other.

Various drawing tools can be used to create and edit strokes and fills and these will be looked at throughout this chapter.

Fills can be plain colours, shades or even coloured lines to create a rainbow effect. These special effects can be particularly useful when creating buttons that the user will press to trigger an interactive function within a movie.

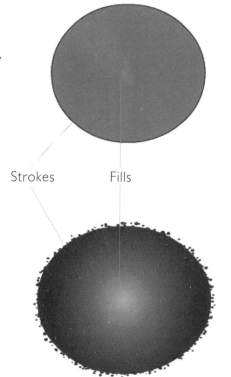

An object with a plain colour fill and the default stroke – a solid black line with a weight of 1

Strokes   Fills

By changing the fill and stroke attributes, the object is changed considerably

Selecting stage level and overlay level objects

Techniques for selecting objects will be looked at in the next chapter but there is one important point to make about selecting solid objects such as circles and squares:

If the fill of a stage level object is selected, it appears shaded. If the stroke is selected it appears as a thick striped line.

- Overlay level objects can be selected by clicking on them once. The object then appears with a solid outline around it. The whole object can then be moved by clicking and dragging

The stroke of an oval stage level object can be selected by clicking exactly on it once. However, only one side of a rectangular stage level object can be selected at a time. To select all sides, select one side, then hold down Shift and select the other three. Or, double click on one side.

An overlay object that has been selected. The whole object can now be moved by clicking and dragging

- Stage level objects are selected by clicking on either the stroke or the fill of the object. This can then be moved in the same way as above, except that only the selected element will move, i.e. either the stroke or the fill. If you want to move the whole of a stage level object, the stroke and the fill have to be selected together. This can be done by clicking above and to the left of the object and drawing a rectangle around the object so that it is all selected. It can then be moved by clicking and dragging

If the fill of a stage level object is selected and moved, it will do so without the stroke, and vice versa. They have to both be selected to move together.

A stage level object selected by clicking and dragging with the Arrow tool from the top left of the object. The whole object can now be moved by clicking and dragging. (This is also how stage level objects are grouped)

The Drawing toolbar

All of the graphics created with the drawing tools are vector-based graphics. This means they are formed by mathematical equations rather than coloured dots (pixels). This gives the images a smoother appearance and they retain their original quality if they are resized.

The Drawing toolbar contains all of the tools needed to created graphics in Flash and they correspond to what you might find in an artist's studio: brushes, pencils, erasers and colour palettes. One of the most useful features of the Drawing toolbar is the modifier section of it. This is a group of additional functions that apply specifically to whatever drawing tool is selected, i.e. the Oval tool has modifiers for the weight, style and colour of the stroke, the fill colour and the gradient of the fill. The modifiers give increased functionality to the drawing tools and enable several editing tasks to be undertaken at once.

The functions of the Text tool are dealt with separately, in Chapter Five.

One of the most useful modifier functions is the option for straightening or smoothing freehand lines. This is looked at in detail in relation to the Pencil tool, on page 48.

Arrow tool — Lasso tool
Line tool — Text tool
Oval tool — Rectangle tool
Pencil tool — Brush tool
Ink Bottle tool — Paint Bucket tool
Dropper tool — Eraser tool
Hand tool — Magnifier tool

Tool modifiers

The modifiers are specific to whichever tool is selected. In this example the modifiers are for the Oval tool. They include stroke colour, weight and style and the fill colour.

Line tool

The Line tool can be used to draw either straight or diagonal lines. It has three modifiers that can be used to set the attributes of lines:

- Line Colour

- Line Thickness

- Line Style

In the Line Thickness box the first option is labelled 'H'. This stands for 'hairline' and it is the thinnest line that can be used.

Click here to select the Line tool

Click here to select the colour palette, to specify the line colour

Click here for the Line Thickness dialog

Click here for the Line Style dialog

The Custom options in the Line Thickness and Line Style boxes let you create your own settings for the Line tool. They both have dialog boxes into which you can enter various attributes for your lines.

To draw lines, select the Line tool, then click and drag on the Stage:

Oval tool

The Oval tool can be used to draw ovals or perfect circles. These can be created with either just a fill, just an outline, or with both. The modifiers for the Oval tool are:

To draw perfect circles, hold down the Shift key while dragging the Oval tool crosshair.

- Line Colour

- Line Thickness

- Line Style

- Fill Colour

The Line Thickness and Line Style dialog boxes for the Oval tool are the same as those for the Line tool.

Click here to select the Oval tool

Click here for the colour palette to select the line colour

Click here to select the line thickness

Click here for the colour palette to select the fill colour

Click here to select the line style

To draw ovals, select the Oval tool, then click and drag on the Stage:

...cont'd

Creating a solid oval
To create an oval with just a fill but no outline:

1 Click here to activate the Line Colour palette

Once the attributes for a particular drawing tool have been set, they become the default settings for all of the other applicable drawing tools. So if you have set the Oval tool to have a line colour of green, thickness 2, and a fill of dark blue, these will be the settings if you then select another drawing tool, such as the Rectangle tool.

2 Click here so an X is showing

3 Select a fill colour and click and drag on the Stage to create the oval

Creating an outline oval
To create an oval with just an outline but no fill:

1 Click here to activate the Fill Colour palette

Rectangles can be created with just a fill or just an outline, in the same way as ovals.

2 Click here so an X is showing

3 Select a line style and click and drag on the Stage to create the oval

Rectangle tool

The Rectangle tool can be used to draw rectangles and squares. Its modifiers are similar to those for the Oval tool:

To draw a perfect square, hold down Shift while you are dragging on the Stage with the Rectangle tool.

- Line Colour

- Line Thickness

- Line Style

- Fill Colour

- Round Rectangle Radius

The buttons next to the Line Colour and the Fill Colour buttons are for the stroke focus and the fill focus respectively. They can be used to specify which part of an object you are selecting the colour for. They can be left alone when choosing colours from the toolbar, but they play a more important role when colours are chosen using the Colours window. This is looked at in more detail in Chapter Five.

Click here for the colour palette to select the line colour

Click here for the colour palette to select the fill colour

Click here to select how rounded the corners of the rectangle are. Enter a value

Click here to select the Rectangle tool

Click here to select the line thickness

Click here to select the line style

Click and drag on the Stage to create a rectangle:

Pencil tool

The Pencil tool is a freehand drawing tool that can be used to create patterns, such as curved lines, or objects such as squares and circles. However, as with most freehand tools in drawing programs, creating objects with the Pencil tool can be an erratic and jerky experience – but only if it is used without any of the assistance that Flash provides for this particular tool. This assistance allows you to specify whether you want your freehand image to be straightened, smoothed or left as it is, with only minor amendments. The other modifiers for the Pencil tool are:

The modifiers for creating straightened or smoothed lines are known as the Pencil Mode modifiers.

*   Line Colour

*   Line Thickness

*   Line Style

When any line is drawn there will be a slight change in its appearance immediately after it has been finished. This is due to Flash ensuring that the finished line will appear as smooth as possible when viewed in the final movie.

Click here to select the Pencil tool

Click here to select the type of assistance for the drawing tool

Click here for the colour palette to select the line colour

Click here to select the line thickness

Click here to select the line style

To create a line with the Pencil tool, click on the Stage and then draw the freehand shape:

Using the Straighten option

To create lines with the Pencil tool that are straight, without any curves:

Lines that have already been drawn can be straightened or smoothed using the Arrow tool. See page 64.

1 Click on the Pencil Mode modifier

2 Select the Straighten modifier

3 Draw a line with the Pencil tool. It will be straightened automatically

The third option on the Pencil Mode modifier is the Ink mode. This does not apply any straightening or smoothing and reproduces the line as it is drawn. This option should be used if no assistance is required when drawing lines and shapes.

Using the Smooth option

To create lines with the Pencil tool that are smooth, without any jagged edges:

1 Click on the Pencil Mode modifier

2 Select the Smooth modifier

3 Draw a line with the Pencil tool. It will be smoothed automatically

Shape recognition only works when drawing circles, ovals and rectangles. If you try to draw a shape such as a triangle, the Pencil tool will try to either straighten or smooth it depending on which settings have been chosen. However, it will not necessarily transform it into a perfect triangle.

Using shape recognition

Not only does the Pencil tool straighten or smooth lines, it can also interpret a particular shape you are trying to draw and create a perfect version of it. This can be invaluable if you are trying to draw items such as ovals and rectangles.

Without shape recognition   Shape recognition applied

Setting assistance levels

There are various options that can be selected to determine the level of assistance given to the drawing tools. To set these levels select File>Assistant from the Menu bar:

Shape recognition works best with the Straighten option selected. If the Smooth option is selected then you could end up with a rectangle with rounded edges. With Ink mode selected, there will be no shape recognition.

- Snap to grid determines how close a line has to be to the grid in order to snap onto it

- Connect lines determines how close the end lines of a rectangle or oval have to be before Flash closes them

- Smooth curves determines the degree by which curves are smoothed

- Recognize lines determines the tolerance for a line before it is automatically straightened

- Recognize shapes sets the tolerance before a shape is turned into an oval or a rectangle

- Click accuracy sets the accuracy for selecting strokes

Brush tool

The brush modes that can be selected for the Brush tool are:

• *Paint Normal, which paints over everything on the selected level*
• *Paint Fills, which paints over fills but not lines*
• *Paint Behind, which paints behind objects*
• *Paint Selection, which paints inside a selected item, and;*
• *Paint Inside, which paints the fill of an item but not the line*

The Brush tool creates broad brush strokes that give the effect of lines being created by actual paintbrushes. The modifiers for the Brush tool are:

•   Brush Mode

•   Fill Colour

•   Brush Size

•   Brush Shape

•   Lock Fill

Click here to select the brush mode

Click here for the colour palette to select the brush stroke colour

Click here to select the Brush tool

Click here to select the brush size

Click here to select the brush shape

While you are using the Brush tool it may appear that it is covering everything on the Stage. However, when you finish using the tool the result will take on the attributes of the selected brush mode.

To use the Brush tool, draw a shape on the Stage as if you were using a paintbrush or a thick crayon. Click and drag to create a line with the Brush tool. You can release the mouse and then draw another line: as long as it is touching the first line, and is the same colour, it will become part of the same shape. This way you can build up complex shapes using a variety of lines. You can even change the brush size and shape halfway through and the new lines will become part of the original object, as long as they are touching it. Brush stokes are objects rather than true strokes.

Ink Bottle tool

The tolerance for how close the ink bottle has to be to a line to change its attributes can be set in the Assistance dialog box. Select File> Assistance. The setting are Strict, Normal or Tolerant.

The Ink Bottle tool can be used to add an outline (stroke) to an object that does not have one, or to change the attributes of an existing outline. This only applies to stage level objects. The modifiers for the Ink Bottle tool are:

* Line Colour

* Line Thickness

* Line Style

Ink bottle attributes can be applied to outlines of elements within an object. However, the new line attributes will only be applied to any elements within the object that can support an outline. For instance, if you had a face graphic and clicked inside it with the Ink Bottle tool, elements such as the eyes, nose and mouth would have the selected outline attributes applied to them.

Click here to select the Ink Bottle tool

Click here to select the line colour

Click here to select the line thickness

Click here to select the line style

To set or change line attributes, select the required line colour, thickness and style. Then position the ink bottle icon over the area where you want to add or edit the line:

Click once here to change or edit a line's attributes

Paint Bucket tool

The Gap Size modifier specifies how the paint bucket fills objects whose outlines are not complete. The settings are:

- *Don't Close Gaps, which prevents a fill being applied to an object with a gap in its outline*
- *Close Small Gaps, which adds a fill to an object with small gaps in its outline*
- *Close Medium Gaps, which adds a fill to an object with medium gaps in its outline, and;*
- *Close Large Gaps, which adds a fill to an object with large gaps in its outline*

The Paint Bucket tool can be used to create a coloured fill within an object, or it can change an existing fill. The modifiers for the Paint Bucket tool are:

- Fill Colour
- Gap Size
- Lock Fill
- Transform Fill

Click here to select the Gap Size

Click here to select the Paint Bucket tool

Click here to select the fill colour

Click here to select the lock fill

Click here to select the transform fill

The gap size tolerance can alter depending on the magnification of the screen.

To use the Paint Bucket tool, select a fill colour and position the paint bucket over the object to be filled or whose fill is to be edited. Click once to add the new fill:

Dropper tool

The Dropper tool only works on stage level objects and it allows you to take the fill or stroke attributes of one item and transfer them to another. It has no modifiers. To use the Dropper tool:

| Select the Dropper tool

If you want to transfer the stroke attributes from one object to another, click once on its outline with the Dropper tool. If you want to transfer the fill, then click once on that.

2 Position it over the fill or stroke that you want to copy. Click once to load the Dropper tool

3 The Dropper tool then activates either the Paint Bucket tool or the Line tool, depending on whether the dropper was loaded with the fill or the stroke of an object

4 Click once on the selected object to transfer the fill or stroke from the original object

Eraser tool

The Eraser tool can be used to delete items on the Stage. It can be used on both strokes and fills, but it can only be applied to stage level objects. The modifiers for the Eraser tool are:

- Eraser Mode

- Eraser Shape

- Faucet

The Eraser tool is activated by selecting it from the toolbar and then clicking and dragging over the Stage. When you are using the Eraser tool it may appear as if it is deleting everything it touches rather than following the specifications of the Eraser mode modifiers. However, when the mouse is released, only the specified elements will have been deleted. (Any other items will reappear.)

Click here to select the Eraser tool

Click here to select the Faucet modifier

Click here to select the Eraser mode

Click here to select the Eraser shape

100%

✓ ○	Erase Normal
○	Erase Fills
○	Erase Lines
⊕	Erase Selected Fills
○	Erase Inside

The Eraser options all have a different impact when they are applied to stage level objects:

Erase Normal

This erases both strokes and fills:

The Faucet modifier for the Eraser tool can be used to delete an entire outline or fill with a single click. Select the Faucet modifier, then click once on a line or fill. This removes it from the Stage.

Erase Fills

This only erases fills, even if the eraser passes over a stroke:

Erase Lines

This only erases strokes, even if the eraser passes over a fill:

Erase Selected Fills

This only erases fills that have first been selected. Everything else is untouched:

If the Eraser tool is applied to overlay level objects, it will have no effect.

Erase Inside

This only erases inside an area without affecting the stroke:

Hand and Magnifier tools

The Hand and Magnifier tools are used to navigate around the Stage and view objects on it at different sizes.

Hand tool

This is used to move around the Stage, without having to use the scrollbars. It has no modifiers.

The Hand tool is a useful way to move around the Stage, but it becomes deselected when another tool is chosen.

Click here to select the Hand tool. Click and drag on the Stage to move around it

Details about viewing options are also given on page 35.

Magnifier tool

This can be used to view the contents of the Stage at different magnifications. It has two modifiers:

- Enlarge

- Reduce

Once the Magnifier tool and its modifier have been chosen, it can be applied by clicking once on the Stage, at the point you want increased or decreased in viewing size.

Click here to select the Magnifier tool

Click here to increase the magnification

Click here to reduce the magnification

Arrow tool

The Arrow tool is the first one on the Drawing toolbar and its purpose is to select objects on the Stage. Some simple selection techniques for stage level and overlay level objects were shown on page 41 and Chapter Four covers some of the other ways to select and then manipulate objects in Flash. The modifiers for the Arrow tool are:

All of the Arrow tool modifiers, except Snap, are only active if an object has already been selected. Otherwise they are greyed out.

- Snap

- Smooth

- Straighten

- Rotate

- Scale

The Snap modifier can be used to align objects with the grid on the Stage.
To show the grid, select View>Grid so there is a tick showing next to it. Objects can then be placed on the lines of the grid and the Snap modifier will ensure that they are aligned exactly on the grid line.

Click here to select the Arrow tool

Click here to select the Snap modifier

Click here to select the Smooth modifier

Click here to select the Rotate modifier

Click here to select the Straighten modifier

Click here to select the Scale modifier

Lasso tool

The Lasso tool is also a selection tool. However, it makes selections by using freehand techniques rather than the point and click or dragging selection employed by the Arrow tool. For instance, it could be used to make a selection of the outline of an open hand. The modifiers for the Lasso tool are:

As with the Arrow tool, the Lasso tool can employ several selection methods and these are looked at in greater detail in Chapter Four.

- Magic Wand

- Magic Wand Properties

- Polygon Properties

The Lasso tool can be used to select segments of stage level objects but not overlay level ones.

Click here to select the Magic Wand modifier

Click here to select the Polygon modifier

Click here to select the Lasso tool

Click here to select the Magic Wand Properties modifier

The Magic Wand modifier can be used so that the Lasso tool can make selections based on the colour of objects. Its settings can be altered using the Magic Wand Properties modifier. This is looked at on page 88.

The Polygon modifier can be used to draw polygon shapes around objects by connecting two points, stopping, and then connecting another two points until the required object has been selected. This can be very useful if you want to select a large, irregular object but your hand is not steady enough to draw around it freehand.

Editing objects

This chapter looks at some of the editing functions that can be applied to drawing objects in Flash. It covers selecting items; editing lines and fills; resizing and reshaping objects; Copy and Paste; aligning items; changing the stacking order; and creating cut-aways.

Covers

Selecting with the Arrow tool | 60

Selecting with the Lasso tool | 63

Editing lines | 64

Grouping objects | 65

Moving objects | 66

Resizing objects | 67

Rotating and skewing objects | 69

Rapid rotation and flipping | 71

Reshaping objects | 72

Copy and Paste | 74

Aligning objects | 75

Stacking order | 77

Cut-aways | 78

Chapter Four

Selecting with the Arrow tool

Clicking and click-dragging

In Chapter Three it was shown how the Arrow tool could be used to select both stage level and overlay level objects and this can be done as follows:

In Flash, an outline is a line that has no end i.e. around an oval or a rectangle. A line, in a Flash context, has a specific beginning and end.

- Click once on an overlay level object to select it

- Click once on the fill of a stage level object to select it

- Click once on the outline of a stage level object to select it

- Double-click within a stage level object to select both the fill and the outline

- Click and drag around either a stage level object or an overlay level object to select the whole object

The Arrow tool can also be used to select multiple objects, of all types, on the Stage by clicking and dragging:

If two or more stage level objects of the same colour are touching, they will all become selected even if only one of the objects is clicked on. For instance, if two squares with a blue fill and no outline were touching they could both be selected by clicking once on either object.

1 Select the Arrow tool

2 Click and drag a rectangle around the items to be selected

3 Release the mouse and all of the items become selected

Stage level object

Overlay level object

To select more than one segment of a line, hold down Shift and click on the segments you want to select. This is the default setting but it can be changed so that multiple segments can be selected just by clicking on them.
To change the default, select File> Preferences from the Menu bar and check off the Selection Options: Shift Select box.

Selecting lines

Since lines in Flash are based on vectors (mathematical equations) rather than being composed of dots, it is possible to select different parts as well as the whole thing. This can be useful if you want to edit one specific part of a line. Lines drawn with the Line tool or the Pencil tool can be selected this way, but only if they are stage level objects. When a line is created in Flash the vector calculation creates a corner point and a curve point for each segment of the line. The curve point is between two corner points and this is the segment of a line that can be select by clicking on it. To select part of a line:

1 Select the Arrow tool; place it at the start of the line. This is the first corner point, denoted by a right angle next to the cursor

Although the Brush tool can be used to create what appears to be lines, these are in fact blocks of colour. You cannot select a segment by clicking on it. However, parts of brush stroke objects can be selected by clicking and dragging – see overleaf.

2 Move the cursor along the line. A small curve will appear next to the cursor, denoting it is a curve point

3 When the cursor finds the next corner point the right angle reappears. This area is a line segment

4 Click once anywhere on the segment to select it

Only stage level objects can have segments selected, not overlay level ones.

Selecting parts of objects

In addition to selecting complete objects and segments of lines, it is also possible to use the Arrow tool to select parts of an object. This can be useful if you want to edit a portion of an object:

When clicking and dragging to select part of an object, position the cursor outside the object to begin the operation. Otherwise you may select the object's fill or outline.

I With the Arrow tool selected click and drag to create the area within the object you want to edit

2 The selected area can now be edited – for instance, changing its colour fill with the Paint Bucket or Brush tools

This technique can also be used to select parts of several different objects:

If selected objects are grouped they become a single item as an overlay level object. For more on grouping, see page 65.

I Click and drag to create the selection area

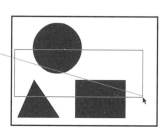

2 The selected objects, or areas of objects, become shaded to indicate they are selected. They can then be edited, grouped or moved

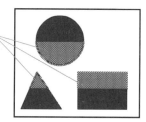

Selecting with the Lasso tool

 Selections with the Lasso tool have to have the same starting and ending point.

While the Arrow tool can be used to select objects by clicking on them or drawing symmetrical boxes around them, the Lasso tool is better for selecting irregular shapes. This can be done by creating a freehand selection or one using the Polygon modifier.

Freehand selection

1 Select the Lasso tool. The modifiers do not have to be selected

 When making a freehand selection, keep the mouse button pressed down until you want to finish the process. If you let go of it before you come back to the starting point, the selection will not be made.

2 Trace around the object to be selected. Finish the selection by double-clicking at the point where you began the selection

Polygon selection

1 Select the Lasso tool and the Polygon modifier

 The Lasso tool can also be used to select colours within bitmap objects. This is looked at in more detail in Chapter Five.

2 Click on a starting point and drag out a line. Release the mouse button where you want the line to end. Repeat this until the whole shape is enclosed by these lines

Editing lines

In addition to using the Pencil, Smooth and Straighten modifiers to create lines with these properties, it is also possible to apply these attributes to lines that have already been created. This is done by using the Arrow tool and its modifiers:

1 Select the Arrow tool and select the line to be edited

If a line consists of more than one segment, double-click on it to select the whole line.

2 Select either the Smooth modifier or the Straighten one

3 Each click on the modifiers produces an incremental change in the line:

Once a line, or line segment, is selected, the Straighten and Smooth modifiers are also available on the toolbar.

After 2 clicks on Smooth

After 10 clicks on Smooth

After 2 clicks on Straighten

After 10 clicks on Straighten

Grouping objects

Groups are always overlay level objects, even if they are made up of only stage level ones.

Several individual objects can be grouped together to form a new, single object. Groups can consist of any objects on the Stage, including stage level objects, overlay level objects, bitmaps and text. Creating groups is useful for applying the same editing technique to multiple items simultaneously, such as moving or resizing. To group objects:

Click on a group once to select it for editing functions such as moving or resizing. Double-click on it to change the attributes of individual elements i.e. fills and outlines. In this mode each element takes on its original properties, within the group.

1 Use the Arrow tool to select the items you want to group, either by shift-clicking or by dragging and drawing around them

2 Select Modify>Group in the Menu bar

3 A thick shaded border appears around the grouped objects

To ungroup an object, select it then select Modify>Ungroup from the Menu bar.

4 Double-click on the group to edit individual items within it. The other items on the Stage are greyed out and the group is identified here

Moving objects

Even if the greatest care is taken when placing objects on the Stage, it is inevitable that most items will have to be moved at some point during the editing process. This can either be done manually or by using the Object Inspector.

Moving manually

Objects can also be moved by selecting them, then pressing the directional arrow keys. This moves the object one pixel at a time. To speed up this process, hold down Shift and press the arrow keys. This will move the object eight pixels each time.

1 Select View in the Menu bar and check on both Grid and Snap

2 Select the object to be moved and drag it to its new location

Moving with the Object Inspector

When using the Object Inspector to move objects it is a good idea to have the rulers showing. This allows you to see the coordinates of where the object is currently situated and also where it will appear once new values have been entered.

1 Select the object to be moved and select Window>Inspectors> Object

2 Enter values in the 'X' and 'Y' boxes to move the object. Check on the 'Use Center Point' box if you want the coordinates to refer to the middle of the object

Resizing objects

As with positioning objects, it is frequently the case that items within a movie have to be resized (also known as scaling in Flash). This could be to increase or decrease an object's prominence on the Stage or to change its proportions in relation to other objects around it. Flash provides three ways to resize objects on the Stage and these apply equally to stage level and overlay level objects.

Resizing manually

If an object is already selected, the resizing function can also be accessed by selecting Modify>Transform>Scale from the Menu bar.

1 Select an object with the Arrow tool (this can include one or more objects)

2 The Arrow tool should still be selected. Select the Scale modifier

Click and drag on one of the resizing handles in the middle of a line to resize the object either horizontally or vertically. Click on one of the corner handles to resize it both horizontally and vertically in equal proportions.

3 Click on one of the eight resizing handles.

4 When a double headed arrow appears, drag to resize the object

If several objects have been selected, they will all be resized proportionally.

Resizing with a dialog box

Resizing using the Scale and Rotate dialog box is a useful option if you want to scale an object precisely. For instance, if you want to make an object half its original size then the most accurate way would be to enter 50% as a value in this dialog box.

The Scale and Rotate dialog box can also be accessed from the Transform Inspector. Select Window>Inspectors> Transform and use the dialog box as above.

1 Select an object and select Modify> Transform>Scale and Rotate from the Menu bar

2 Enter a percentage value for the increase/decrease amount. Select OK

Resizing with the Object Inspector

1 Select an object and select Window> Inspectors>Object

2 Enter values here for the new width and height for the object

3 Click Apply for the new setting to become active

Rotating and skewing objects

An object can be rotated (moved to varying degrees around its centre point) or skewed (distorted at various angles along its horizontal or vertical axis). The operations for doing this are similar to those for resizing objects and they can be applied to stage level or overlay level objects. However, overlay level objects can be rotated in a slightly different fashion (see the tip).

Stage level objects are always rotated around their actual centre point, which remains static. However, the centre point of overlay level objects can be moved, to change the point from where the rotation is applied.
To do this, select an overlay object, then select Modify>Transform>Edit Center from the Menu bar. A thick cross appears in the middle of the object. Click and drag to move it around the object and set a new centre point.

Rotating manually

1 Select an object and select the Arrow tool and the Rotate modifier

2 Click on one of the corner rotating handles and drag the object to its new position (dragging one of the side handles will distort the object i.e. skew it)

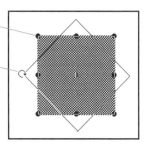

Rotating with a dialog box

1 Select an object and select Modify>Transform>Scale and Rotate, in the same way as for resizing an object

2 Enter a value for the amount you want the object to be rotated

Skewing with Inspectors

1 Select an object and select Window> Inspectors>Transform from the Menu bar

The Transform Inspector can also be used to rotate objects. Check off the Skew box and the options for Rotate are reduced to one box. Enter a value here to rotate the object by a selected number of degrees.

2 Enter horizontal or vertical values for skewing the object and make sure the Skew box is checked on

3 The skew effect makes the object look misshapen

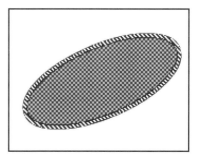

Rapid rotation and flipping

Objects can be re-orientated quickly by rotating them left or right by 90 degrees or flipping them 180 degrees horizontally or vertically. To do this:

The Transform menu also has an option for undoing any resizing or rotating commands that have been applied to objects, but only overlay level ones. To do this, select an overlay level object, then select Modify>Transform>Remove Transform from the Menu bar. The object will now revert to its original state.

This is similar to the Undo option but it can be quicker if several editing commands have been applied, since it takes the object back to its original state in one step.

Select an object and select Modify> Transform and any of the following commands:

- Rotate Left
- Rotate Right
- Flip Vertical
- Flip Horizontal

Original   Rotate Left   Rotate Right

Flip Vertical   Flip Horizontal

Reshaping objects

Both lines and fills can have their shapes altered, which can be a useful way of manipulating items and creating some interesting freehand effects. When reshaping objects there are three important points to remember:

- You can only reshape stage level objects

- When you are reshaping lines or fills you do not have to select them first. If you do you will move the item rather than reshape it

- Both lines and fills in Flash are made up of corner points and curve points. The corner points are at the end of lines or at a point in a line or fill that Flash calculates is at a sufficient angle. Corner points are denoted by a small right angle next to the cursor when it passes over one. These can be used to reshape the corner of fills or the end of lines. Curve points are denoted by a small curve next to the cursor. These can be used to reshape the middle of fills or lines.

Reshaping a straight line

In Flash, any points between the two corner points of a straight line are considered to be curve points, even though they are completely straight.

1 Select the Arrow tool and position it over one end of the line, without selecting the line. A small right angle will appear next to the cursor

2 Click and drag to stretch and reposition the line

Reshaping a curved line

1 Select the Arrow tool and position it over part of the line, without selecting it. A small curve will appear next to the cursor

It is possible to add corner points to fill objects. This gives increased flexibility when reshaping objects and means that corner points can even be added to objects such as perfect circles.

To create corner points: select the Arrow tool and position it over a curve point so the small curve is showing. Hold down Ctrl+click (Windows) or Alt+click (Mac) and then drag the cursor. As it is dragged the object will be reshaped and a new corner point will be created.

2 Click and drag to reshape the curve

Reshaping a fill

1 Select the Arrow tool and position it over either a corner point or a curve point of the fill object

2 Click and drag to reshape the fill

Reshaping using corner points

Reshaping using curve points

Copy and Paste

Copied items can be pasted back into the location they came from as well as a new frame, layer, scene or movie.

In common with many software programs, Flash offers the standard Copy, Paste and Cut facilities. In addition, it has an option for pasting objects into the same relative position as they were copied from. The Copy and Paste functions are particularly useful for copying or moving items between frames, layers and scenes. They can also be used to move items from one movie to another.

Standard Copy and Paste

Edit>Cut can be used in the same way as Edit>Copy. However, this removes the item from its original location, but it can still be pasted somewhere else.

Select the item to be copied

2 Select Edit>Copy from the Menu bar

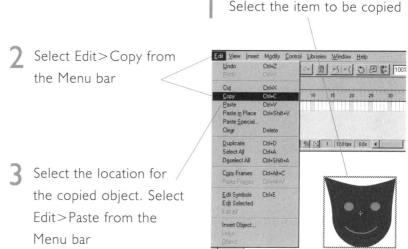

3 Select the location for the copied object. Select Edit>Paste from the Menu bar

Using Paste in Place

Paste in Place is an excellent option if you want to have various items in exactly the same place throughout a movie. This could include items such as company logos or menu bars.

To paste an object in the same relative position, measured from the top-left corner of the Stage, from where it was copied:

Copy the object as above, choose a location for it, then select Edit> Paste in Place from the Menu bar

Aligning objects

Even with the grid and ruler options, it can be useful to have a function for aligning a number of objects in one operation – for instance if you want to line up a group of buttons as navigation tools. Flash provides this with a number of alignment options for both stage level and overlay level objects.

Alignment options

Within the Align dialog box there are a number of options that can be selected. To align objects:

| Select the objects to be aligned

In addition to aligning objects vertically and horizontally, the Align dialog box also has options for matching the width and height of the largest object in the selection.

2 Select Modify>Align from the Menu bar

Text can be aligned using the same method as for objects.

3 Select the required alignment options from the Align dialog box (see overleaf)

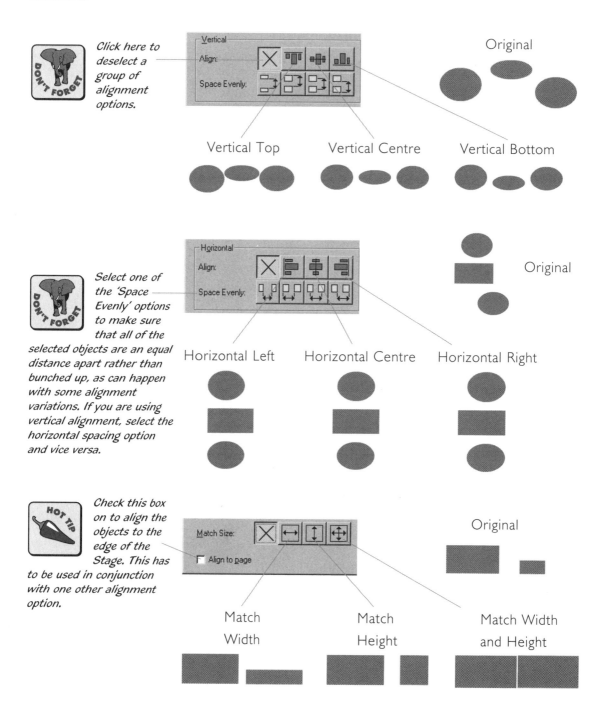

Click here to deselect a group of alignment options.

Original

Vertical Top   Vertical Centre   Vertical Bottom

Select one of the 'Space Evenly' options to make sure that all of the selected objects are an equal distance apart rather than bunched up, as can happen with some alignment variations. If you are using vertical alignment, select the horizontal spacing option and vice versa.

Original

Horizontal Left   Horizontal Centre   Horizontal Right

Check this box on to align the objects to the edge of the Stage. This has to be used in conjunction with one other alignment option.

Original

Match Width   Match Height   Match Width and Height

Stacking order

As movies are created, the number of objects on the Stage increases. This is generally not a problem if the objects are apart, but when they start to overlap it can become an issue. For instance, if you have an image of a person kicking a ball, it is important to have the ball showing in front of the individual rather than behind them. This is known as stacking, and Flash enables you to arrange objects in a variety of ways.

Only overlay objects can be arranged: if you have a stage level object that you want to arrange it has to first be grouped or turned into a symbol (see Chapter Six).

To arrange overlay level items:

1 Select the object whose stacking order you want to change

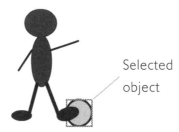

Selected object

2 Select Modify>Arrange from the Menu bar and select one of the stacking options

3 The stacking order of the selected object changes accordingly

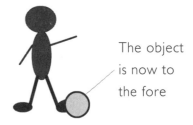

The object is now to the fore

Cut-aways

If two stage level objects with the same fill or outline colours are placed over each other they will not be able to be used for cut-aways. Instead they will merge into one object: any matching colours in stage level objects that touch, join together as one.

The reason stage level objects cannot be stacked is because they physically affect each other when one is placed on top of another. In this way, one stage level object can be used to create cut-aways from another. This can be done with either objects or lines.

Cut-aways with objects

1 Draw two stage level objects, one on top of the other

2 Select one object and click and drag it to see the cut-away effect

Cut-aways with lines

If you try to use a stage level object to cut away an overlay level one, nothing will happen. Since the overlay object is, in effect, on a different level the stage level one will just appear behind it and no interaction will take place.

1 Draw a stage level object. With either the Line or the Pencil tool, draw a line across it. This divides the object into two distinct segments

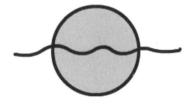

2 Select one of the segments and click and drag it to see the effect of the cut-away

Colour and text

Both colour and text can be used to give extra dimension to a Flash movie. This chapter looks at adding colours and gradients to objects, creating new colours and gradients and selecting colours. It also shows how to add, format and manipulate text.

Covers

Standard Colour palette | 80

Adding solid colours | 81

Adding gradients | 83

Editing gradient fills | 85

Colour focus | 87

Selecting colours | 88

Adding text | 89

Formatting text | 91

Manipulating text | 92

Chapter Five

Standard Colour palette

When the Colour Line or Colour Fill box is chosen for a drawing tool the standard Flash Colour palette appears. This has a selection of the most commonly used colours and it contains two elements:

Any of the applicable drawing tools can be loaded with fill or gradient colours. Select the tool you want to use and then select an option from the Colour palette. This will stay in place for any other drawing tools, until another selection is made.

- *Solid colours.* Solid blocks of colour

- *Gradient colours.* Bands of colours that merge into each other to give a gradient effect. Gradient colours can either be radial gradients, which uses rings of colours to create the gradient effect, or linear gradients, which uses lines of colours

Radial gradients are excellent for items such as buttons on a Web page. The gradient gives the button greater depth and creates a more interesting 3-D effect.

Click here to select a solid colour fill

Click here to select a radial gradient fill

Click here to select a linear gradient fill

Adding solid colours

Computer monitors create colours by mixing different amounts of red, green and blue (the RGB colour model). In theory this can produce over 16 million colours. However, not all computer monitors can display this number of colours. The maximum number guaranteed to be displayed correctly is 256 (or only 216) and this is known as the Web Safe Colour palette.

If you use colours outside this range some monitors will interpret them as best they can, but they may differ from the original. This is known as 'dithering' and it usually results in inferior colour representation. If in doubt, stick to Web Safe colours, which are the ones Flash uses by default.

Since not everyone wants to be restricted to just the colours within the standard Colour palette, Flash has an option for creating new colours and adding these to the Colour palette. This gives an almost limitless range of colours from which to choose, but if these are intended for a Web page, it is worth remembering that they may not necessarily be displayed on the user's browser exactly as intended (see the tip).

To create a new solid colour:

1 Click here on the Colour palette to access the Color dialog box

2 Select a colour in the Solid Color dialog box

Click here to select a colour

Colour preview

Check this box on to create the nearest Web Safe colour to your selection

Create a colour by adding RGB (Red Green Blue) values here

Hexadecimal is a system that uses six digits to denote colours. It works by giving values for red, green and blue, using a base system of sixteen. This uses the numbers 0–9 and the letters A–F. Each of the three colours (Red, Green and Blue) used to create a hexadecimal colour has a combination of two letters/ digits assigned to it.. For instance, white is FFFFFF and black is 000000. There are 256 (16x16) hexadecimal combinations, matching the Web Safe palette.

3 Edit the chosen colour:

Edit a colour's hue and saturation by clicking and dragging this crosshair

Create a colour by checking this box on and entering hexadecimal values in the RGB boxes

Edit brightness by clicking and dragging this slider

Edit transparency by clicking and dragging this slider or by entering a value

If the Alpha setting for a colour (its transparency) is at 100% then it will be at its most dense. If it is at 0% it will be completely transparent i.e. invisible.

4 Select New to add the new colour to the Colour palette

5 Select Change to apply changes to an existing colour. The new or edited colour is then added to the Colour palette

Adding gradients

Gradients can be added and edited in a similar way to solid colours. This is done by selecting which colours will make up the gradient and how thick each band of colour will be.

To create a new gradient:

In addition to accessing the Colour palette by selecting a drawing tool and then selecting the Fill or Line Colour box, it can also be displayed by selecting Window>Colors from the Menu bar.

1 Click here on the Colour palette to access the Color dialog box

2 Select the Gradient Color dialog box

3 Click here to select either a linear or a radial gradient

Gradients can produce very effective fills for items such as buttons.
However, try not to overdo this effect and use gradients carefully.

4 The colours that make up the gradient are shown here. Click once on one of the pointers to edit a particular colour in the gradient. This can be done in the same way as for defining solid colours

Colours can be removed from gradients by clicking and dragging a gradient pointer off the scale.

5 Drag the colour pointers along the Gradient Definition bar to alter their relationship in the gradient. The results are shown in the Preview box

Gradients must have a minimum of two colours. If more colours are used this allows for either dramatic effects to be created with different colours or greater subtlety to be achieved by using several shades in the gradient.

6 Add more pointers by clicking and dragging here. The more pointers, the more flexibility there is for editing the gradient

7 Select New to add the gradient to the Colour palette

or

Select Change to apply changes to an existing gradient

If Delete is selected in the Gradient Color dialog box, it will remove the selected gradient completely.

Editing gradient fills

Gradients can be applied to objects in the same way as solid colours: select a drawing tool such as the Oval or Rectangle tool, select the Fill box and choose a gradient from the Colour palette. Alternatively, the Paint Bucket can be used to change the gradient of an existing stage level object. It is also possible to use the Paint Bucket tool to edit existing gradient fills.

Moving a gradient's centre point

1 Select the Paint Bucket tool and the Transform Fill modifier from the Drawing toolbar

2 Select the object whose gradient you want to edit

3 Click and drag the centre point to change the position of the gradient

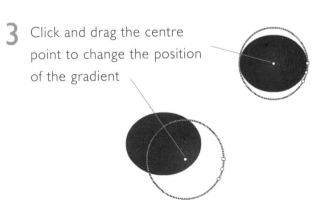

Changing a gradient's shape

Three small buttons appear around a gradient fill when it is selected. These are on the right hand side of the object and are, from top to bottom:

- *Change Gradient Shape*
- *Change Gradient Radius, and;*
- *Change Gradient Rotation*

1 Select the Paint Bucket tool and the Transform Fill modifier as on the previous page and select the object to be edited

2 Click and drag on the Change Gradient Shape button to make the gradient larger or smaller

Changing a gradient's radius

1 Select the Paint Bucket tool and the Transform Fill modifier as above and select the object to be edited

2 Click and drag on the Change Gradient Radius button to make the gradient's radius larger or smaller

Applying rotation to a gradient has no effect unless its centre has already been moved, as on the previous page, or its shape has been changed.

Changing a gradient's rotation

1 Select the Paint Bucket tool and the Transform Fill modifier as above and select the object to be edited

2 Click and drag on the Change Gradient Rotation button to rotate the gradient

Colour focus

For objects that have both a fill colour and a line colour, such as rectangles and ovals, the colours can be determined by the relevant colour modifier for each option i.e. the Line Colour and the Fill Colour palettes. However, there is a time-saving device where both colours can be chosen without having to switch between the Fill and the Line boxes. This is done by using the Colour Focus buttons, which are located to the right of the Line Colour and Fill Colour boxes. To add colours using the focus buttons:

Once the Stroke or Fill Focus button has been selected, the Color dialog box can also be accessed by clicking on the Line or Fill Colour box and selecting the Color dialog box button from the top of the palette. This is the same as for creating solid or gradient colours – see page 81.

1 Select the Oval or Rectangle drawing tool and select the Stroke Focus button

2 Select Window>Colors from the Menu bar

3 Create a new colour in the Color dialog box or edit an existing one

4 Select the Fill Focus button. The Color dialog box will remain active and the fill colour can then be created or edited

Selecting colours

Solid colours can be selected with the Arrow tool or the Lasso tool. However, this is not always effective if you want to select areas of colour within a bitmap image i.e. a photograph. To do this, the Lasso tool can be used in conjunction with its Magic Wand modifier:

1 Import an image and break it apart so that individual areas of colour can be selected (see the DON'T FORGET tip)

2 Select the Lasso tool and the Magic Wand modifier

3 Select the Magic Wand Settings modifier and enter the relevant settings

4 Select an area of colour on the bitmap by clicking on it once with the Magic Wand tool

Adding text

In Flash, text can be more than just plain words on the screen. It can serve this purpose perfectly well, but it can also be used to create animations. These will be dealt with in Chapter Nine. However, it is important to look at the basics of text entry. Two points to remember:

- Text is created as an overlay level object, so it is placed on top of any stage level objects on the Stage

- In its original format text is created in text labels or boxes. These can be edited and formatted in a similar way to text in a word processing program. However, text can also be broken apart so that individual words and letters can be used as shapes and formatted accordingly

The text modifiers can also be selected from the Menu bar. Select Modify and then either Font, Paragraph, Style or Kerning. Kerning is the amount of space between individual letters. The options are Narrower or Wider and this can be applied by inserting the cursor between the individual letters whose kerning you wish to change and then applying the required command.

Text can be added as text labels or text boxes.

To add a text label

Select the Text tool, then carry out the following as appropriate:

Click here to select a font

Click here to apply a colour

Click here to select an alignment

Click here to select a font size

Click here to select Bold and/ or *Italic*

Click here to select paragraph properties

Text labels can be used to position specific words at the end of a line. **Press Return** *after the required word, and a new line will be started underneath it.*

2 Click on the Stage with the Text tool. Enter the text into the text label

3 The text will continue along the Stage, and

A text label will keep expanding

eventually off the edge into the Work Area, unless Return is pressed to create a new line

To add a text box

1 Follow Step 1 on page 89

A text label is denoted by a small circle in the top right hand corner of the box into which the text is typed. A text box is denoted by a small square.

2 Click and drag the text crosshair on the Stage to create a text box of a specific width

3 When the text is entered it will wrap (move to the next line down) when it exceeds the width of the text box. The text will expand downwards, increasing the height of the text box, but the width will remain constant

Text in a text box will wrap downwards, expanding the box.

Formatting text

General formatting

Text can be aligned in either a text label or a text box by inserting the cursor within a paragraph and selecting the Alignment modifier. The options are Left, Center, Right or Justify. To align more than one paragraph at a time, click and drag to select all of the text to be aligned.

1 With the Text tool, select the text by clicking and dragging the cursor over it

2 Select options from the Text tool modifiers, as with creating text on page 89

3 The text displays the selected choices:

Paragraph formatting

For paragraph properties, line spacing is always measured in a default of points. The margin and indent measurements default to the settings applied to the ruler. This can be changed by selecting Modify>Movie and entering a new unit of measurement in the Ruler Units box.

1 Select a paragraph and select the Paragraph modifier

2 Enter settings in the Paragraph Properties dialog box:

The distance between the text and the text label or box container

The amount the first line of each paragraph is indented

The amount of space between lines

Manipulating text

When rotating text, the greatest impact can be achieved by rotating individual words or letters. If too much text is rotated the effect is lost and it becomes difficult to read.

In addition to standard formatting for text, it can also be manipulated as if it were a graphic, rather than plain text.

Rotating and resizing

As with graphical objects, words or letters can be rotated and resized:

1. With the Arrow tool select a word or letter by clicking on it once

2. Click the Rotate modifier to rotate the text by clicking and dragging on a corner handle

or

Click the Resize modifier to resize the text by clicking and dragging one of the resizing handles

After text has been broken apart it may still be selected, which is denoted by shading over the affected area. Deselect the text by clicking anywhere away from it on the Stage. Then select the Arrow tool and move it over the text to reshape it. However, make sure not to select the object itself.

Reshaping text

Text can also be reshaped like a graphical object:

Reshaping objects is covered in Chapter Four, pages 72–73.

1. Select a letter or word and select Modify > Break Apart from the Menu bar

2. Click and drag either a corner point or a curve point to reshape the text

Symbols and instances

Flash has a function for creating an object once and then using it numerous times, without significantly increasing the size of the movie file. The two items used for this are called 'symbols' and 'instances'. A symbol is a master object which can be reused numerous times to create copies (instances) on the Stage. This chapter looks at creating and editing symbols and instances. It also looks at the Library, which is the area where symbols are stored.

Covers

Symbols and instances defined | 94

The Library | 96

Creating symbols – the conversion route | 100

Creating a new symbol | 102

Symbol Editing Mode | 104

Editing symbols | 105

Duplicating symbols | 106

Editing instances | 107

Chapter Six

Symbols and instances defined

Symbols and instances play a vital role in ensuring Flash's ability to create graphic-intensive movies, while still maintaining file sizes small enough to achieve an acceptably fast downloading time. Symbols are reusable items and they can consist of animations, static graphics, text or interactive buttons. An instance is created from a symbol and when it is placed on the Stage it appears identical to the symbol from which it was created. So an instance of a star graphic would look exactly like its symbol, at least when it is first placed on the Stage.

Whenever a symbol is created it is automatically placed in the Flash Library. This is an area for storing the items that are used in a particular movie – see page 96.

However, although instances look as if they are straight copies of the original symbols they are in fact only *references* to the symbol. This means they are not actually objects in their own right and so take up virtually no file space. So, a dozen instances could be created from one symbol and the amount of file space taken up would be only a little more than that occupied by the original symbol. This is invaluable if you want to use the same object numerous times in a movie. In addition, instances do not have to look exactly like the symbol from which they were created: it is possible to change their size and colour to give the effect of several different objects, while still referring them back to one original symbol.

Although individual instances can be edited independently of the original symbol and any other instances created from it, if the symbol is edited these changes will affect all of the instances of it on the Stage.

Six instances created from one symbol. Each instance has been edited by either recolouring, resizing or rotating but they all still refer back to the original symbol

Types of symbols

There are three types of symbol, each of which can be used for certain functions. In addition, there are two other items that act in a similar way to symbols, even though they do not technically fall into this category:

Symbol types are also known as behaviours i.e. how the symbol reacts when it is placed in a movie.

- *Graphics.* These are the objects that are created with the Flash drawing tools. Not all graphics have to be turned into symbols and if it is an item that is only going to be used once, and remain static throughout the movie, then there is little point in changing it into a symbol. However, if a graphic is going to be reused throughout a movie, or even used in another movie, then it is worth turning it into a symbol. This operation is very quick and can save a lot of time and effort

Symbols have their own timelines that run independently of a movie's main Timeline. This is particularly important for button and movie clip instances since it gives them greater flexibility in the way they relate to the main movie i.e. a movie clip could be playing even though the main Timeline has stopped.

- *Buttons.* These are interactive objects that perform an action when they are pressed by the user. They can be programmed to perform a number of actions and these are looked at in detail in Chapter Ten

- *Movie clips.* These are animations that are placed within a movie. They are self-contained animated objects which can be used multiple times in a movie. Movie clips are a powerful and flexible way to create impressive animated effects and they are looked at in detail in Chapter Nine

- *Bitmaps and sounds.* Several types of bitmap images and sounds can be imported into Flash. They are then treated like symbols and the equivalent of instances can be created from them

Once symbols have been created they are placed in the Library. Before looking at how to create symbols it will be useful to look at the function of the Library and how it deals with symbols. This is covered on the following pages.

The Library

The Library is the storage area where the content of a Flash movie is contained. All of the elements of a movie can be kept here and symbols are placed here automatically when they are created. They are then dragged from the Library onto the Stage to create instances.

Accessing the Library

| If the Library is not already showing, select Window>Library from the Menu bar

2 Select an item and it will be displayed in the Preview window. The items in the Library are displayed here with an icon depicting their type

3 Click here to expand the Library window. This gives fuller details about each item stored in the Library

Click here to return to the standard Library window

When you first start creating a Flash movie you may think it is unnecessary to create numerous folders. However, the number of items you want to store in the Library will soon increase and folders are a good way to organise them.

Creating new folders

One of the main functions of the Library is as a management system for all of the reusable items in a movie. In this respect it is similar to a file management system such as Windows Explorer in Windows or Finder on the Mac. As with these, it is possible to create folders and sub-folders for storing items. To create a folder:

1 At the point where you want to insert a new folder click here on the Library window

2 The folder name will be highlighted as 'untitled folder 1'. Type a new name for the folder

If new folders are created in the main Library window these are known as root folders. These could be used for items entitled 'animations', 'buttons' and 'graphics'.

Folders can also be created inside other folders and these are known as sub-folders. These are created by double-clicking on an existing folder and creating a new folder as normal.

Deleting items

All objects within the Library can be deleted, including entire folders:

1 Select the item to be deleted and click here on the Library window

2 A warning dialog box appears to check that you really want to delete this item. Click Delete

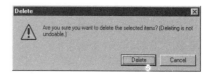

The Library menu

Some of the functions of the Library, such as creating new folders and deleting items, can be accessed from icons within the Library. Other functions are accessed from the Library Options menu:

Click here to sort items in the Library. This can be done by Name, Kind, Use Count (the number of times an item has been used in a movie), or Date Modified, depending on which heading is selected. Maximise the Library window to view all of the column headers.

Click here to access the Library Options menu

Items in the Library can be moved from one folder to another by dragging and dropping. Select the item you want to move. Click and drag it until it is over the folder into which you want to put it and release.

The functions on the Library Options menu are:

- *New Symbol*. This creates a new symbol. (Symbol creation is covered on pages 100-103)

- *New Folder*. The same as using the new folder icon

- Rename. Enables the selected item to be renamed

- *Move to New Folder*. Creates a new folder and moves the selected item into it

- *Duplicate*. Makes a copy of the selected item. This can be useful if you want to change a symbol's properties i.e. change a graphic into a button, but still maintain the same appearance for the item

- *Delete*. The same as using the Delete icon

If you have a Library collection from one movie and you want to use some of the items in another movie you can do so by copying and pasting the items individually between the two files. However, there is a much quicker way: opening another Library into the current movie.

Select File>Open as Library and the Open as Library dialog box will display all of the movies that have already been created. Select one and select Open. This movie's Library will become available in the current movie and all of its contents can be used.

- *Edit*. Enables a symbol's properties to be edited

- *Properties*. Displays the selected item's properties i.e. its name and whether it is a graphic, a button or an animation

- *Select Unused Items*. Selects all of the items that have not been used in the movie. These can then be deleted as a batch by clicking on the Wastebasket icon. This is a good way to remove redundant items

- *Update*. This updates any editing changes that have been made to an imported item

- *Play*. This plays sounds, movie clips or buttons in the Library

- *Expand Folder*. This expands the selected folder to view all of its contents. This can also be done by double-clicking on the folder

- *Collapse Folder*. This collapses the selected open folder so none of the items in it are visible. This can also be done by double-clicking on the open folder

- *Expand All Folders*. This expands all of the folders in the Library

- *Collapse All Folders*. This collapses all of the folders in the Library

- *Keep Use Counts Updated*. This automatically updates the counter for the number of times each item in the Library has been used. This can be seen if the Library window is expanded to its full size

- *Update Use Counts Now*. This updates the use counter if Keep Use Counts Updated is not checked on

Creating symbols – the conversion route

Symbols can be created by two methods:

- Converting existing items into symbols

Frames are looked at in greater detail in Chapter Eight.

- Creating symbols from scratch (this is done in Symbol Editing Mode) and then adding content

All three types of symbols (graphics, buttons and movie clips) can be created using either method but the preferred option is different depending on the type of symbol being created:

Buttons and movie clips are created in Symbol Editing Mode. This has all of the same facilities as for creating items on the main Stage. Once the symbol editing process has been completed the item (along with its own timeline and frames) can be placed on the main Stage.

- Since graphic symbols do not require any animation or interactivity they do not have to be edited beyond their initial state i.e. a single frame. Therefore they can be converted directly into symbols

- Buttons and movie clips both require more than one frame's worth of content and so it is best to create a blank symbol and then add all of the content from scratch

Converting objects into symbols

1 Select the required objects on the main Stage. These can be stage level objects, overlay level object, text, groups or other symbols

2 Select Insert> Convert to Symbol from the Menu bar

...cont'd

If you do not give symbols names when they are created you will end up with several similarly named items, which could become confusing.

3 Type a name for the symbol. The default will be something like Symbol 7 (or the next sequential number for the symbols that have been created)

4 Select the type of symbol to be created (its behaviour). Select OK

An instance can also be created from the Library by clicking and dragging the symbol's name onto the Stage, rather than the image in the Preview window.

5 The symbol is placed in the Library and displayed in the Preview window

If an instance is deleted from the Stage it will not affect the symbol in the Library. However, if a symbol is deleted from the Library, all instances of it on the Stage will also be deleted.

6 Click and drag the symbol to create an instance of it on the Stage

Creating a new symbol

For button or movie clip symbols it is best to create them from scratch using the New Symbol function. They can be created by converting an item into a symbol and then adding any additional elements that are required for the interactive button or the animation. However, since it can become slightly complicated as to what is a symbol and what is an item on the main Stage, it is probably best to stick to this method for buttons and movie clips.

Graphics can also be created from scratch using this method.

There are three ways to begin creating a new symbol from scratch:
Select Insert>New Symbol

or

Access the Library Options menu by clicking here, and selecting New Symbol

or

Click the New Symbol icon in the Library

When a new symbol is created it is automatically placed in the Library once OK is selected in the Symbol Properties box. The content of the symbol can then be added, or it can be added (or edited) at any time in the future. See page 105 for more information about editing symbols.

Each method accesses the Symbol Properties dialog box. Enter a name and select a behaviour for the symbol you want to create. Select OK

Creating button symbols involves creating four different states for the button:

- *one for before it has been activated (Up)*
- *one for when the mouse cursor passes over it (Over),*
- *one for when it is clicked on (Down), and;*
- *one for the area around the button that can activate its functions (Hit).*

Button symbols are looked at in more detail in Chapter Ten.

3 Symbol Editing Mode is then accessed. This is the environment in which the symbol will be created. This is the Symbol Editing Mode for creating a button

Symbol Timeline   Symbol Stage

This is the environment for creating a movie clip. It looks the same as the main Stage environment, but it is actually the movie clip symbol's own individual stage and timeline

Movie clip symbols can be used independently on the main Stage. However, they can also be inserted into graphics, button symbols and even other animations. Movie clips are looked at in more detail in Chapter Nine.

4 The symbol is added to the Library as soon as it has been created, even if no content has been added at this point

Symbol Editing Mode

Since new symbols are created with their own stage and timeline it can sometimes become confusing as to whether you are working on the main Stage or in Symbol Editing Mode. However, it is possible to identify in which mode you are working and switch between the two:

You have to double-click on the symbol icon in the Library and not the symbol name to access Symbol Editing Mode. If you double-click on the name this will just highlight it, so that its name can be changed by overtyping.

1 To open a symbol in Symbol Editing Mode, double-click on the symbol icon in the Library

or

Click here at the right-hand side of the toolbar to access a list of the symbols in the movie. Select one from the drop down list

Scenes can be used to divide a movie up into manageable chunks, which is particularly useful if you are working with very large movies. Scenes are looked at in more detail in Chapter Nine.

2 The name of the active symbol is displayed here. This denotes you are working in Symbol Editing Mode

3 Click on the scene name to return to the main Stage

or

Click here and select a scene to move to

Editing symbols

Once changes have been applied to a symbol these will be applied to all instances of the symbol that have already been placed on the Stage. So if a circle symbol is changed to a square, all of the circle instances will become squares too.

Once a symbol has been created it can still be edited to change both its properties and its appearance. Its appearance can be altered by editing it in Symbol Editing Mode. In addition to the methods in Step 1 on the facing page, Symbol Editing Mode can also be accessed as follows:

• Select an instance of the symbol on the Stage. Select Edit>Edit Symbols from the Menu bar

• Select an instance of the symbol on the Stage. Select Edit>Edit Selected from the Menu bar

• Select a symbol in the Library. Select Edit from the Library Options menu (click on the small arrow next to Options to access the menu)

• Select a symbol in the Library and then double-click on the image in the Preview window

If you want to edit a symbol in its actual environment on the Stage, right-click (Windows) or Ctrl+click (Mac) on it and select Edit in Place from the contextual menu that appears. This allows you to edit the symbol while still viewing the relationship between it and the objects around it. The other objects are visible but greyed out while the editing takes place.

• Double-click on an instance on the Stage. This activates the Instance Properties dialog box. Select a symbol and click here to edit it

Once a symbol is in Editing Mode it can be modified in the same way as any other object. In this case a graphic symbol has been edited by reshaping with the Arrow tool

Duplicating symbols

When using symbols there may be occasions when you want to use the same item for a different purpose. For example, you could have a graphic that remains static throughout your movie, except for one part when you want to animate it for added impact. It is possible to create a graphic symbol and then go through the whole creation process again, only this time assigning a movie clip behaviour to the symbol and editing it accordingly. However, it is much quicker to create a duplicate of the original symbol and then edit its content. To do this:

1 Select a symbol in the Library and select Duplicate from the Library Options menu

 If a duplicate symbol is not assigned a name when it is created it is given the same name as the original but with 'copy' after it.

2 In the Symbol Properties dialog box, type a name for the duplicate symbol and select a behaviour. Select OK. At this point the duplicate will have exactly the same appearance as the original. If it has been assigned a different behaviour it can then be edited accordingly i.e. a movie clip can be animated or a button can have interactivity added

Editing instances

When instances are dragged onto the Stage from the Library they are overlay level objects.

As shown on page 101, instances are created by selecting a symbol in the Library and dragging it onto the Stage. The object on the Stage is always an instance and the symbol itself never appears outside the Library (although it is possible to edit a symbol by accessing one of its instances on the Stage).

Individual instances can have their size, rotation and colour properties edited and this does not affect the symbol from which they were created, or other instances from the same symbol.

Resizing and rotating

It is possible to edit the size and appearance of an instance, but if you want to change its content this has to be done to the original symbol in Symbol Editing Mode. This alters the symbol and any instances of it on the Stage.

If you want to create objects based on the same symbol but with different sizes and orientations this can be done by resizing and rotating individual instances:

1 With the Arrow tool, select an instance on the Stage

When instances are dragged onto the Stage, they are placed in the nearest keyframe. For more on frames and keyframes, see Chapter Eight.

2 Select either the Rotate or the Scale modifier from the toolbar and rotate or resize using the handles that appear

Editing colour properties

It is possible to edit an instance's colour in a number of ways: changing its brightness, tint, and transparency. To edit an instance's colour:

When instances are selected on the Stage they appear with a thick shaded box around them and a cross in the middle.

1 Double-click on an instance or select it and select Modify>Instance from the Menu bar

The Special option in the Color Effect dialog box can be used to set the tint and transparency values simultaneously.

2 In the Instance Properties dialog box, select the Color Effect tab. Click here to access the options:

Brightness. Increase or decrease it by entering a value or dragging the slider on the right

In the Tint dialog box, the Tint Amount option determines the level at which the selected colour is applied. If it is at 0% the original colour will be unaffected. If it is at 100% the selected colour will be applied in full.

Tint. Create a new colour by entering RGB values, selecting a colour or accessing the Colour palette

In the Alpha dialog box, 0% in the Alpha option makes an object completely transparent.

Alpha. Sets how opaque/transparent an object is. Enter a value or drag the slider

Bitmaps and sound

In addition to creating drawing objects within Flash it is also possible to import bitmap images, such as photographs, and sound files. This chapter looks at how to import and edit both of these items and shows how they can be used to enhance a Flash movie.

Covers

Using bitmaps | 110

Importing bitmaps | 111

Bitmap properties | 112

Tracing bitmaps | 113

Bitmaps as fills | 114

Using sound | 117

Importing sounds | 118

Editing sounds | 119

Chapter Seven

Using bitmaps

Bitmaps are images that are created by using pixels (tiny coloured dots) to represent the image. Although Flash uses a different method to create graphics (vector-based, using a mathematical formula) it can support certain bitmap formats and it is possible to incorporate them into a movie.

Hard copy images such as graphics or photographs can be converted into bitmaps by using a scanner. This creates a digital image which can then be imported into Flash, providing it is created in an acceptable format.

Images taken with a digital camera can also be imported into a Flash movie.

Using bitmap images has a number of advantages:

- More complex images such as photographs can be used

- Bitmaps can be used as stand-alone images or they can be incorporated into backgrounds or fills

- There is greater opportunity for creating eye-catching content

The main drawback of bitmaps is that they generally take up more disk space than vector-based graphics, which adds to the size of a Flash movie and so has an adverse effect on the all-important downloading time. However, there are techniques that can be used to compress the size of bitmaps when they are incorporated in Flash movies.

Types of bitmaps

There are dozens of different formats for bitmap images. The ones that are supported by Flash are:

It is also possible to import graphics from other vector-based programs such as Macromedia Freehand or Adobe Illustrator.

- BMP (Windows only)

- PICT (Mac only)

- JPEG (Windows and Mac)

- GIF (Windows and Mac)

- PNG (Windows and Mac)

Images in these formats can be imported into Flash and used in their original format. In addition to this, they can also be broken apart to allow for standard Flash image editing functions to be applied to them.

Importing bitmaps

Once a bitmap has been created it can be imported into a movie from your hard drive, from an external storage device such as a Zip drive, or from a digital source such as a digital camera or a scanner. To import a bitmap:

If you want to import a bitmap directly from an external device, select this location at the top of the Import dialog box and then select the bitmap.

1 Select File>Import from the Menu bar

2 Locate the bitmap you want to import. Select Open (Windows) or Add>Import (Mac)

When importing bitmaps, Flash will only display files whose format is supported by the program.

3 The bitmap is placed on the Stage and a copy is also placed in the Library. Although this is not strictly speaking a symbol, copies of the bitmap can be made by dragging it onto the Stage from the Library

Bitmap properties

When a bitmap is imported into a movie one of the most important issues is its file size. This is determined by the images resolution i.e. the number of pixels in the image. The higher the resolution then the larger the file size. This is measured in dots per inch (dpi) and if you are creating bitmaps for use in a Flash movie it is best to set the dpi to a maximum of 72. This is because computer monitors generally cannot display more than 72 dpi, so anything of a higher quality will be wasted and just lead to an unnecessarily large file size.

When a bitmap has been imported into a movie it is possible to edit some of its properties so that it appears at the highest quality but with the smallest file size. To edit a bitmap's properties:

1 Double-click on a bitmap in the Library (or click on it once and select Properties from the Library Options menu)

2 Edit the settings in the Bitmap Properties dialog box:

Preview window

Allow smoothing – check this on to give the image a smoother appearance

Compression options – determines how an image is compressed, thereby decreasing its file size

Tracing bitmaps

It is possible to turn bitmaps into vector-based graphics by using a technique called tracing. This can give greater flexibility when it comes to editing the bitmap. To trace a bitmap:

Tracing bitmaps can be a hit and miss affair and it can take a few minutes for the vector image to be produced.

1 Place a copy of the bitmap on the Stage and select it

2 Select Modify > Trace Bitmap from the Menu bar

3 Enter values in the Trace Bitmap dialog box:

To get the best results when tracing photographs it is necessary to set:

- *a low colour threshold*
- *a small minimum area*
- *a tight, or very tight, curve fit, and;*
- *a normal corner fit.*

However, this can greatly increase the file size of your movie.

- *Color Threshold*. This determines how much each pixel has to differ in colour from the one next to it for a new vector calculation to take place. A higher threshold means fewer calculations. The settings are between 1 and 200

- *Minimum Area*. This determines how many neighbouring pixels are included in calculating the colour. This can be between 1 and 1000

- *Curve Fit*. This determines how closely a vector image follows the original. The settings are: Pixels, Very Tight, Tight, Normal, Smooth and Very Smooth

- *Corner Fit*. This determines whether the vector image creates smooth or sharp corners. The settings are: Many corners, Normal and Few corners

Bitmaps as fills

Once a bitmap has been imported into a movie it can be used as an individual image or it can be used as a fill for objects, in the same way as solid colours and gradients. To use a bitmap as a fill:

Once a bitmap has been broken apart, it becomes a stage level object and takes on the appropriate properties.

1 Select a bitmap on the Stage. Select Modify>Break Apart from the Menu bar

The Lasso tool and Magic Wand modifier can be used to select colours within a broken apart bitmap.

With the relevant tools selected, click on an area of colour on the bitmap. Depending on the Magic Wand properties, an area of colour will be selected, which can then be used as a fill. This technique is also covered on page 88.

2 The bitmap becomes shaded, indicating that it has been broken apart

3 Draw an object on the Stage that is going to be filled with the bitmap

4 Select the Dropper tool from the Drawing toolbar and click once with it on the broken apart bitmap

Once a bitmap fill has been chosen this becomes the default for all drawing objects, until another fill is selected.

5 The tool turns into the Paint Bucket. Click inside the drawing object to add the bitmap fill

Editing bitmap fills

A bitmap fill is created using an image with the same dimensions as the original bitmap. This is fine if the object to be filled is the same size as the bitmap. However, if it is smaller then only a small amount of the bitmap may appear and if it is larger the bitmap will be tiled i.e. the image will be repeated in a tile pattern. However, it is possible to edit bitmap fills once they have been applied to a drawing object:

Tiling can produce some interesting effects for both drawing objects and backgrounds. Experiment with different images to see how they appear when tiled.

1 Select the Paint Bucket tool and the Transform modifier. Click within the drawing object that contains the bitmap fill. The Fill Transform box appears around the bitmap that was clicked on

Make sure the bitmap-filled drawing object is deselected before you click on it with the Paint Bucket and Transform modifier.

2 Click and drag the centre point to move the position of the bitmap within the object

If a drawing object is too small for the bitmap fill, only one area will be visible in the object. The fill can be resized using the options on this page so it is all visible in the object. However, it may then be too small to be viewed properly.

3 Click and drag the horizontal and vertical resizing handles to make the fill larger or smaller

4 Click and drag the horizontal skew handle to skew the fill accordingly

5 Click and drag the vertical skew handle to skew the fill accordingly

HOT TIP

The button at the bottom left corner of the Transform Fill box is the Proportional Resize button. This resizes the fill horizontally and vertically in equal proportions.

6 Click and drag the rotation handle to rotate the fill left or right

Using sound

Sound in Flash

In addition to its array of visual functions, Flash can also utilise sound files to give an extra dimension to a movie. These files have to be created outside Flash and then imported into a movie. They can then have some basic editing techniques applied to them. The two sound formats that can be used in Flash are:

Flash comes with a selection of its own prerecorded sounds. Select Libraries>Sounds from the Menu bar to access them. These libraries also contain buttons, graphics and movie clips.

- .WAV (Windows)

- .AIFF (Mac)

When a sound has been imported into a movie it can be used as:

- *An event-driven sound.* These are sounds that play when a certain action is performed, such as an interactive button being pressed. Event-driven sounds have to be downloaded completely before they play and the sound plays in its entirety before stopping, regardless of what else is happening in the movie

- *Streamed sounds.* These are sounds that are synchronised with the content of the movie, such as a soundtrack for a specific piece of animation. Streamed sounds are downloaded as each piece is required so even if it is a long sound file the user will be able to start listening to it before the whole clip has downloaded

Most clip art collections on CD-ROMs also have libraries of sound clips.

Creating sounds

Sounds can be created using a simple sound recorder such as the ones that come with most Windows operating systems (Sound Recorder) and Mac (SoundSimple). There are also numerous CD-ROMs that have sound collections on them, or you could try the following Web sites:

- http://www.webplaces.com/html/sounds.htm

- http://www.wavcentral.com/

Importing sounds

Sound files cannot be created directly within Flash so they have to be imported from the hard drive or an external storage source. To import a sound:

1 Select File > Import from the Menu bar

2 Locate the required sound file and select Open (Add > Import on the Mac)

Once a sound has been imported and placed in the Library, it can be inserted into a movie by clicking and dragging it onto the Stage. The sound file will be placed on the selected layer at the nearest keyframe (see Chapter Eight for more information about layers and frames).
Select Control>Test Movie to hear the sound play or select the Play arrow in the Library Preview window.

3 The sound is placed in the Library automatically. A digital representation of the sound is displayed in the Preview window

Click here to hear a selected sound

Editing sounds

A keyframe is denoted by a solid or hollow dot on the timeline.

When working with sound files, create a new layer for each one. This will keep all of the sound files separate and make them easier to work with. For more information on layers, see Chapter Eight.

When editing the volume of a sound, increase or decrease it by the same amount for each channel. Otherwise, when the sound is played there will be different sound levels for the left and right speakers.

Once sounds are in a movie, some simple editing techniques can be applied to them:

Changing the volume

1 Double-click on the keyframe that contains the sound. A small portion of the sound will be visible in the keyframe

2 Select the Sound tab in the Frame Properties dialog box. The sound file will be displayed. The top window is for the left channel of the sound and the bottom window is for the right channel

3 Click and drag here (the envelope handle) to move the line (the envelope line) to increase or decrease the sound accordingly

Fading sounds in

Fading in and out is a useful technique for introducing sounds subtly, rather than suddenly.

Select a sound on the Stage and open the Frame Properties Sound dialog box (see the previous page). Drag the envelope handle to the base of the window.

Click the envelope line to add a new handle and drag this to the top of the window. This will cause the sound to fade in

Changing the start and end point

The time-in and time-out controls determine how much of a sound is cut off i.e. the whole of the sound is not played, just the portion between the two buttons.

Click and drag here on the time-in button to make the sound begin at a different point. The same can also be done for the end point of the sound

Sound Frame Properties

Click here to preview a sound and any effects that have been added to it.

Click here to apply special effects

Click here to display the sound timeline in frames rather than seconds

Click 1 of these to zoom in or out

Frames and layers

Frames and layers are two important items for adding and controlling content in a movie. This chapter looks at inserting and editing frames and layers and how they can be used to simplify the editing process of a movie.

Covers

Working with frames | 122

Adding frames | 125

Deleting and copying frames | 127

Frame properties | 128

About layers | 129

Working with layers | 130

Inserting layers | 131

Deleting and copying layers | 132

Layer modes | 133

Layer properties | 134

Mask layers | 135

Chapter Eight

Working with frames

The terminology of frames and keyframes comes from the days when all animations were drawn by hand.

The keyframes were the ones where a specific event occurred in the animation, such as a character turning its head, and the regular frames were the ones where there was only static content. These frames were known as in-between frames i.e. the frames in-between where the actual animation took place. This is where Flash takes one of its main animation terms from – tweening. This is the technique for adding frames in between two keyframes in an animation.

(Tweening is looked at in Chapter Nine.)

Frames are the components of a movie that allow content to be added on the Stage. They also play a vital role in creating animations. There are different types of frames but they all serve the same basic purpose: to control the way content is displayed and viewed in Flash.

Keyframes

The most significant type of frame is a keyframe. This is like a master frame that denotes there has been a change in the content on the Stage. Every Flash movie is opened with an empty keyframe inserted in the first frame of the movie:

An empty keyframe, i.e. one with no content added on the Stage, is denoted by a hollow circle

Once content has been added to the Stage, the circle becomes filled

Frames can also have actions added to them (such as 'stop playing the movie' or 'move to a particular frame'). A keyframe that has had an action added to it is denoted with a small 'a' above the keyframe circle:

Actions can be added to keyframes to give them increased interactivity. See Chapter Ten for more on this

Once content has been added to a keyframe, this will remain visible on the Stage until another keyframe occurs:

To move between keyframes and regular frames click and drag on the Playhead.

The content in the keyframe of frame 1 on the Timeline is a circle. Since another keyframe does not occur until frame 5, the circle will remain on the Stage until that point

Keyframes are placed within the blank frames on the Timeline.

The speed at which frames are played in a movie (the frame rate) can be set by selecting Modify> Movie from the Menu bar and then entering a value in the Frame Rate box in the Frame Properties dialog box. The default is 12 frames per second, which is considered best for display on the Web.

The content in the keyframe of frame 5 on the Timeline is a square. At this point, the circle that appears in the first four frames will disappear and the square will replace it

Some points to remember about keyframes:

- Keyframes have to be added if you want to create animations or include interactivity

- All movies have to have at least one keyframe

- All movies begin with a blank keyframe already inserted in frame 1 of the Timeline

If a new keyframe is inserted with no regular frames preceding it, these frames will be inserted automatically.

Regular frames

Regular frames contain the content of the nearest preceding keyframe and they can be used to determine the distance between keyframes and also the overall length of a movie. Regular keyframes are denoted by solid shading on the Timeline:

On the Timeline, the compartments with neither a keyframe nor a regular frame are known as blank frames.

Setting movie length with frames

A movie will not play beyond the last frame on the Timeline, whether it is a regular frame or a keyframe. In this way it is possible to set the length, in frames, of a movie. If you want a movie that is 20 frames long, then insert a regular frame or a keyframe at that point. (See the facing page for details on adding frames.)

Creating a background with frames

The background to a movie is a static element that can remain in place for the whole movie, allowing other objects to be placed on top of it.

When creating a background for a movie, place it on its own layer and position this layer at the bottom of any others in the movie. This will ensure that the background is always behind any other items on the Stage. For more on layers, see page 129 onwards.

1 Create your background in the keyframe in frame 1

2 Insert a regular frame at the point where the movie will end. The background will occupy all of these frames

Adding frames

Regular frames and keyframes can be added at any point within a movie.

Adding regular frames

1 Select a blank frame on the Timeline where you want the new frame added

A regular frame can be added within a group of existing regular frames. Select a regular frame and then add a frame as described on this page. This inserts a new regular frame to the right of the one that was selected. This can be done to extend the duration an item remains on the Stage during the movie. This increases the playing time of a movie.

2 Select Insert>Frame from the Menu bar, or right-click (Windows), Ctrl+click (Mac), and select Insert Frame

3 A regular frame is inserted and takes on the content of the nearest preceding keyframe

Adding keyframes

Keyframes should be added whenever you want to create a change in a movie. This could be a visual change, or the inclusion of an action that performs a certain task within the movie.

1 Select a frame on the Timeline where you want the new keyframe inserted

2 Select Insert>Keyframe (or Blank Keyframe) from the Menu bar, or right-click (Windows), Ctrl+click (Mac), and select Insert Keyframe (or Insert Blank Keyframe)

If you only want to make small changes between the content in successive keyframes, then the new keyframe option is the best one. If you want to make significant changes then it may be better to insert a blank keyframe and build the content from scratch.

3 A new keyframe has the same content as the preceding keyframe. This can be edited accordingly for the new keyframe

4 A new blank keyframe has no content, until items are added to the Stage in this keyframe

Deleting and copying frames

Deleting frames

Both regular frames and keyframes can be deleted from any point on the Timeline:

If a keyframe is deleted, all of its contents will be removed and replaced by the content in the preceding keyframe.

Select the regular frame or keyframe. Select Insert>Delete Frame or Insert>Clear Keyframe

Copying frames

Frames can be moved from one layer to another by selecting them and then dragging them between layers.

1 Select a single frame by clicking on it on the Timeline, or select a range of frames by clicking on the first frame and then dragging over the range to be selected on the Timeline

2 Select Edit>Copy Frames from the Menu bar

When a range of regular frames is copied, the preceding keyframe is also inserted at the point where the frames are pasted on the Timeline.

3 Select the frame where you want the copied frames to be placed. Select Edit>Paste Frames from the Menu bar

Frame properties

Various properties can be assigned to frames. These include those for animation (Tweening) and interactivity (Actions), which are looked at in Chapters Nine and Ten respectively. Sound files that are located in a particular frame can also be edited in the Frame Properties dialog box. A fourth option is for adding labels and comments to a frame. A label is an identifier that is used to locate specific frames within a movie when working with interactive elements. Comments can be added as reminders about the content of a frame. They do not affect the published movie and are for information only in the editing environment. To add labels and comments:

Labels and comments can be added to regular frames and keyframes, but if they are added to regular frames they always appear at the nearest preceding keyframe.

Double-click on a frame to open the Frame Properties dialog box. Enter a name in the Name box and select Label or Comment as the Behaviour

Comments can be used as reminders to do certain things during the editing process. This could include a comment to add a particular item to a frame or to start an animation at a certain point.

A label is denoted on the Timeline by a red flag and the name of the label

A comment is denoted on the Timeline by two green strokes and the name of the comment

About layers

Layers are an organisation device in Flash that allows you to separate the content of a movie into manageable sizes. Layers act like sheets of glass placed one of top of another. Content can be added to each sheet and when they are compiled all of the content on the layers can be viewed together. Some points to remember about layers in Flash:

Use a new layer for each new element you add to the Stage.

- The order of layers is called the stacking order

- Content in the bottom layer that is covered by the next layer will not be visible, and so on through all of the layers

- It is possible to change the stacking order of layers

- When creating a new item (such as a drawing object, an animation, a bitmap, a sound or an interactive button) it is a good idea to place it on a new layer. This will make it easier to edit and it means you will not have any other items getting in the way

It is possible to hide the content of layers. This is useful if you want to work on a layer without being distracted by the content on other layers. See page 133 for details about hiding layers.

- Only one layer can be selected and worked on at a time

- The background of a movie should always be on a separate layer, at the bottom of the stacking order

- Layers can be given their own individual names

- Dozens of layers can be added to a single movie

- When a movie is published, Flash displays the content in frame 1 of all of the layers used. It then displays the content in frame 2 of all of the layers and so on

It is possible to lock layers so that the content cannot change by accident.

- Layers can have their own stacking order if they contain stage level and overlay level objects. This internal stacking order is preserved if the layer is moved within the overall stacking order

Working with layers

The order in which objects appear in a movie can be changed by altering the position of its layers.

If no content overlaps on any layers then it may seem unnecessary to worry about the stacking order of them. However, if more content is added to any of the layers this could affect objects on other layers and the stacking order may have to be adjusted accordingly.

The layers of a movie are displayed here.
The top layer (triangle) is the one that appears as the foremost on the Stage. If it covers other objects, or parts of objects, behind it then these items will not appear. Similarly the second layer (square) covers some of the object in the third layer and this is not visible

When moving a layer, a thick shaded line appears when you click and drag it. Place this above or below another layer to move it into this position.

Click and drag a layer to move its position in the stacking order. This changes the relationship between the objects on the Stage. In this case the Circle layer has been moved to the top, so the circle moves to the front on the Stage and covers the items behind it

Inserting layers

If you select an item on the Stage that is on a different layer from the one currently being edited, the layer of the selected object will become the active one. This way, you can move between layers by clicking on different items on the Stage.

All new movies are opened with one layer (entitled Layer 1), a Timeline and a blank keyframe in frame 1. Additional layers can be added at any time during the editing process and they also have a blank keyframe in frame 1. New layers can be inserted at any point in the stacking order of existing layers. To insert new layers:

1 Select the layer above which you want to insert the new layer

2 Click here to add a new layer or select Insert>Layer from the Menu bar

A layer can be renamed at any time, by double-clicking on its name and overtyping.

3 To rename the new layer, double-click on its name and overtype a new one

Layers do not add to the size of a movie. The content is the thing that adds to the file size, so you can use as many separate layers as you like.

4 Enter content for the new layer. This will appear on the Stage according to the layer's position in the stacking order

Deleting and copying layers

Deleting layers

If you decide you do not want to use the contents of a layer, it can be deleted from the movie:

If you delete a layer and its contents by mistake, select Edit>Undo from the Menu bar immediately after you have performed the delete operation. The Undo function in Flash only applies to the immediately preceding editing action.

| Select the layer to be deleted. Click the Wastebasket icon to remove it

2 The layer is removed from the stacking order and its contents are deleted from the Stage

Copying layers

If you want to use the same, or similar, content from one layer, this can be copied and pasted into a new layer. This is done with the Copy Frames and Paste Frames commands as shown on page 127:

| Insert a new layer in the stacking order

2 Select all of the frames in the layer to be copied and then copy and paste them into the new layer. The new layer will take the same name as the one from where the content was copied

Layer modes

Only one layer can be the currently selected one. However, any layer can be placed in hidden, locked or Outline Mode and it does not have to be selected first.

Layers have four modes that can be selected, to make it easier when working with multiple layers:

Current Mode. This is the active layer on the Stage and is denoted by a pencil icon next to the layer name

Hidden Mode. This hides the contents of the selected layer and is denoted by a red cross in the column below the eye

Locking layers is a good way to ensure the content is not edited by mistake.

Locked Mode. This locks the contents of the selected layer so it cannot be edited and is denoted by a padlock in the column below the padlock icon

Outline Mode allows you to see the outlines of all of the layers on the Stage and can be a useful way of viewing how different objects overlap on different layers.

Outline Mode. This displays the contents of the selected layer as outlines only and is denoted by a coloured square in the column below the square

Individual layers can have Hidden, Locked or Outline Modes applied to them. Also, all layers in a movie can have these modes applied by clicking on the icons at the top of the columns

Layer properties

Various attributes within a layer can be determined in the Layer Properties dialog box:

The Layer Properties dialog box can also be accessed by right-clicking (Windows) – or Ctrl+clicking (Mac) – on a layer and selecting Properties from the contextual menu that appears.

1 Select a layer and select Modify>Layer from the Menu bar

2 Select options for the layer's properties:

Double-click here and overtype to change the layer name

Click here to make the layer content visible or locked

In addition to normal layers there are also Guide and Mask layers. Guide layers are used to help control an animation's movement (see Chapter Nine). Mask layers are used to hide certain parts of other layers (see the facing page).

Click here to select the type of layer (see the HOT TIP)

Click here to choose a colour if the layer is displayed in Outline Mode

Click here to determine the height of the layer. The default is 100% but it can be changed to 200% or 300%, useful for viewing sound files in a layer

Mask layers

Mask layers are a special type of layer that works in a similar way to a stencil. A Mask layer can have objects added to it and it is then placed on top of another, regular layer. The content of the regular layer will only be visible through the content of the Mask layer: the rest of it masks the regular layer and hides any other objects. There are two important points to remember about Mask layers:

- Regular layers have to be linked to Mask layers for the mask to function

- The content of the regular layer will only be visible through the area on the Mask layer that has content. Although the mask content may look as though it is covering the regular layer, the reverse is true. The content on the Mask layer acts like a window, allowing the content behind it to be visible

Once the concept of Mask layers is fully understood they can be used to create some highly artistic effects. It is an area that is worth persevering with and experimenting with.

Creating a Mask layer

When adding content to the layer that is going to be the Mask layer (in this case the layer in Step 2) it does not matter about its colour. This is because when it is acting as a mask the objects will be completely transparent to allow the content below it to show through.

1 Create a regular layer and add content

2 Add a new layer above the first layer and add content. Make sure it covers some of the content in the first layer

A Mask layer can be linked to several regular layers.

3 Select the layer that will be the Mask layer

Mask layers are always above any regular layers which are linked to them. To link a regular layer to a Mask layer, click and drag the regular layer until the shaded line connected with the regular layer is directly below the Mask layer. Release and the regular layer becomes linked to the mask one.

To unlink a layer, click and drag it away from the Mask layer.

4 Right-click (Windows) or Ctrl+click (Mac) and select Mask

A Mask layer is denoted by a circle with a down pointing arrow inside it and a linked layer is denoted by a circle with a right pointing arrow

5 The Mask layer is now linked to the regular layer below. On the Stage the content on the regular layer is only visible through the content on the Mask layer

RINGS

Animation

This chapter looks at the animation techniques that can be used in Flash. It shows frame-by-frame animation and also how to move objects using motion tweening and how to change one shape into another using shape tweening. It also looks at animating text and creating movie clips.

Covers

Animation basics | 138

Elements of animation | 139

Scenes | 142

Frame-by-frame animation | 144

Motion tweening | 147

Motion guides | 150

Motion guide orientation | 151

Shape tweening | 152

Animating text | 155

Movie clips | 156

Chapter Nine

Animation basics

Animation in Flash is, in many respects, just a technologically advanced version of traditional hand-drawn animation. In the days before computers, animations were created by drawing thousands of pictures and then playing them in sequence to create the animated effect. To reproduce the impression of movement, numerous drawings of an object were made, with each one slightly different from the preceding one. In this way the animators were able to create moving objects and characters using the same basic images.

In addition to creating moving objects, some items in an animation are static, such as the background. This difference helped form the hierarchy between the animation artists: the more highly paid and experienced ones created the moving items in an animation and the less well paid or less experienced artists usually stuck to the less technical drawings. This meant that there were groups of artists working on different layers within the same scene of animation. When all of the layers were collated, the final animation appeared.

In many respects Flash uses the same techniques as hand-drawn animations: objects can be animated on one layer, while other layers can contain elements that remain static throughout the movie. There are two types of animation that can be performed in Flash:

- *Frame-by-frame animation.* This is a form of animation where an object's appearance or position is changed slightly from frame to frame to create the impression of movement. This involves using a new keyframe for each change and it can be a time-consuming process

- *Tweened animation.* This is where you select the starting and finishing points for an object and Flash animates it by filling in all the frames in between (hence the name). Motion tweening (moving objects) and shape tweening (changing the shape of objects) can both be applied

Elements of animation

The Timeline

The Timeline is the collection of layers and frames that contain the content of a movie. It can also be used to control how objects are animated. The default Timeline shows the layers, frames and keyframes in the movie. However, this can be amended to show the information in other formats:

| Click here to change the way frames are displayed on the Timeline

The Short option shrinks layers vertically. Use this if you want more layers to be visible at a time.

2 Choose a setting for how the frames are displayed

Tiny

If Tinted Frames is checked on then all regular frames and keyframes will be tinted.

Large

3 Click here to view the objects in each frame on the Timeline

Preview in Context shows the content for each frame but in the context of its actual size on the Stage.

Timeline status bar

At the bottom of the Timeline is a status bar that contains important information about the movie:

Current frame being viewed

Time elapsed to reach current frame (in seconds)

Fps during playback

The Playhead

The Playhead can be used to move between frames to view their contents. When the Playhead is positioned over a frame, all of the content at that point is displayed:

Click and drag the
Playhead to move
through a movie. If
this is done

reasonably slowly it will display the results of any frame-by-frame animations, as the Playhead displays the contents of each frame in turn

Onion skinning

When creating an animation it can be a great help to see what the objects in the preceding and succeeding frames look like. This way it is possible to make any subtle amendments to the item you are working on so it will fit in smoothly with those around it. This is known as onion skinning and can be used as follows:

1 Create an animation. In this example it is a simple motion tween of a ball moving across the Stage

2 Select a frame in the animation. Click here to activate onion skinning

3 The object in the selected frame and the two before and after it are displayed

4 Click and drag here to extend the number of frames that are included in the onion skinning

5 Click here to view the onion skinning in outline format

6 Click here to access the Modify Onion Markers menu. The bottom three options determine how many frames are affected by the onion skinning

Scenes

When working with scenes it may feel as if each one is a separate entity. But each scene is part of the overall movie. All scenes have the same properties as each other i.e. those defined in the Movie Properties dialog box (accessed by selecting Modify>Movie from the Menu bar).

Scenes in Flash are similar to their namesakes in a play: they are created separately but they are an important sequential part of the overall production. Scenes can be used to break up long movies into more manageable sizes, with different parts of the movie being broken up into separate scenes. For instance, if you have a movie that begins in an external location and then moves to an internal one, this could be broken up into two scenes. When using scenes it is worth remembering a couple of points:

- When creating a new scene, there is no evidence of other scenes in the editing environment, so if there are elements that are required throughout the whole movie, these will have to be recreated in the new scene

- Scenes play sequentially in the order they are created. However, it is possible to rename and reorder scenes in movies

Adding a new scene

New scenes can be inserted from the Menu bar or the Scene Inspector:

If you have a background that will appear throughout the movie, copy it from Scene 1 and then paste it as the bottom layer in any subsequent scenes.

1 Select Insert>Scene from the Menu bar

2 The name of the active scene is shown here

...cont'd

or:

Select Windows> Inspectors>Scene

To delete a scene, select it in the Scene Inspector and click on the Delete button. This will remove the scene and all of its contents.

2 Click Add in the Scene Inspector to add a new scene

To reorder the sequence in which scenes play in a movie, click and drag on a scene in the Scene Inspector. Move it within the scene structure and then release. The movie will now play the scenes in this order.

Renaming a scene

Scenes can be given unique names, which makes it much easier when working with numerous scenes:

In Scene Inspector, double-click on a scene or click on it once and select the Properties button

To move between scenes, access the Scene Inspector and select a scene. Also click on the Edit Scene icon at the right-hand side of the toolbar:

Click on the arrow to select a scene.

2 Type a new name for the scene in the Scene Properties box. This is the only action that can be performed in this dialog box. Select OK

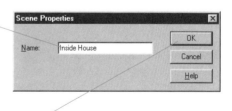

Frame-by-frame animation

A frame-by-frame animation involves inserting keyframes for each change in the animation and then editing the content accordingly. This way you are specifying the content for each frame of the animation: it is similar to drawing images on separate pages in a book and then flicking through it to create the animated effect. Frame-by-frame animations can be as simple or as complicated as you like, but the more complicated, then the longer it will take to edit the content for each frame.

Several different objects can be animated at the same point in a movie. Use layers for each individual element that is going to have animation applied to it.

Creating a simple frame-by-frame animation

To create an animation of a ball bouncing across the screen:

I   Open a new movie by selecting File>New. Create a background on the existing layer. Insert a regular frame at frame 20

Objects can be drawn in the Work Area rather than the Stage for the first keyframe of an animation. This will give the effect of the object 'flying in' from off the screen rather than starting on the Stage. A similar effect can be created for the end of an animation by placing the content of the final keyframe in the Work Area.

2   Insert a new layer above the background one and make sure the Playhead is at frame I

3   At frame I, select the Oval tool and draw a circle on the Stage (give it a fill colour but no outline; this will make it easier to work with)

To make it easier to position objects when you are creating frame-by-frame animations, turn on the grid by selecting View>Grid from the Menu bar.

4 Select frame 5. Select Insert>Keyframe from the Menu bar. The ball will still be in the same position as it was in frame 1

Once objects have been positioned in a keyframe it is possible to reposition them at any time in the editing process, by clicking on the relevant keyframe.

5 Click and drag the ball and move it to a new position on the screen

If you are creating complex animations such as people walking, draw each part separately i.e. the head, the body and the limbs. This is because in some keyframes certain parts may not move. Static elements, such as the body, can be reused, while the moving parts can be repositioned.

6 Insert new keyframes at frames 10, 15 and 20 and reposition the ball each time as in Step 5.

7 Select Control>Test Movie (or Test Scene) from the Menu bar to see the animation's progress. At this point it may look rather crude and jerky

To change the speed at which an animation plays (the frames per second speed) select Modify>Movie and change the value in the Frame Rate box. A higher value speeds up the animation and a lower figure slows it down. The Frame Rate box can also be accessed by double-clicking on the Frames Per Second (fps) box on the Timeline:

12.0 fps

With this example the animation will keep playing indefinitely in its current state. In order to stop it once the ball reaches the end of its path, a stop action has to be inserted at frame 20. This is looked at in Chapter Ten.

8 To smooth out the animation, select the frames between the keyframes that have already been inserted i.e. 2–4, 6–9 etc. Insert a keyframe into each one and reposition the ball slightly each time. Click on the onion skinning button to see how the position of the ball in each keyframe relates to those around it

9 When all of the keyframes have been added and the ball repositioned, the path of the ball can be seen by stretching the

onion skinning markers across the length of all of the frames used. Select Control>Test Movie (or Test Scene) to see the animation in action

Motion tweening

Motion tweening can create similar results to frame-by-frame animation, except it is usually quicker because Flash does a lot of the work for you.

Motion tweening is an animation technique that involves denoting the starting and ending point of an animation and then instructing Flash to fill in all of the frames in between. Only symbols, groups and text blocks can be used for motion tweens, but if a simple drawing object is required to be used in this way, Flash automatically converts it into a symbol. Motion tweens are excellent for depicting movement and a number of different properties can be defined, for additional creative power. To create a motion tween:

Only symbols, groups or text blocks can be used in a motion tweening animation.

1 Select File>New to open a new movie. In frame 1 add a drawing object

2 Move to frame 20 on the Timeline. Insert a new keyframe and reposition the object

To insert a keyframe, select Insert> Keyframe from the Menu bar – alternatively, right-click (Windows) or Ctrl+click (Mac) – and select Insert Keyframe from the contextual menu.

3 Select frame 1 again and select Insert>Create Motion Tween

If you use the Playhead to view an animation this will not be at the same speed as when viewed in the testing environment or when it is published.

4 An arrow now spans the frames

between the two keyframes. This denotes that a tween has been created

5 View the animation by clicking here on the controller; dragging the Playhead from

frame 1 to frame 20; or selecting Control>Test Movie (or Test Scene) from the Menu bar

Turn on onion skinning to see how Flash has inserted the in-between frames for the animation.

6 If the object that was used for the motion tween was originally a simple drawing object, it will have been converted into a symbol, inserted into the Library and given a name such as Tween 1. However, this is just a normal symbol and it does not contain any animated elements within it. Rename these symbols as soon as they are created

Editing a motion tween

Motion tweens can be edited so that the animation changes size, rotation and colour during the course of the tween. To apply editing techniques:

If these editing changes were applied to the motion tween in the example, it would begin small and transparent and then fade into view, increase in size and rotate 90 degrees. Effects like these can be used to give motion tweens a lot more versatility.

1 Select frame 1 and select the object with the Arrow tool. Select the Resize modifier from the Drawing toolbar. Resize the object by clicking and dragging one of the resizing handles

2 Double-click on the object in frame 1. In the Instance Properties dialog box, select Color Effect>Alpha. Set the Alpha setting to 0%.
This will make the object completely transparent to start with and it will then fade in as it moves

Using the Alpha setting to make objects transparent is a popular technique for making graphics and text fade in and out of a movie.

3 Select frame 20. Select the object with the Arrow tool and select the Rotate modifier. Rotate the object by clicking and dragging on the rotation handles

Motion guides

Motion Guide layers are always above any regular layers to which they are linked. A linked layer is recognisable on the Timeline because it is indented below the Guide layer.

In a basic motion tween, the object moves in a straight line between the starting and ending keyframes. In addition to this, it is also possible to create a freehand path for the object to follow as it moves between its starting and ending points. This is done with a device called a motion guide and it can be inserted as follows:

1 Select the layer containing the motion tween. Select Add Guide Layer

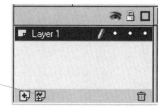

2 The Guide layer is inserted above the layer containing the motion tween (now linked to the Motion Guide layer)

More than one layer can be linked to a Guide layer. Click and drag the required layer and place it below the motion guide. The object on this layer will follow the motion guide path.

3 Select the Pencil tool in the Drawing Toolbar and the Smooth modifier. Draw a freehand line joining the start and end points of the object

For each new motion guide path you want to create, a new Motion Guide layer has to be inserted.

4 The motion tween will follow the path of the line

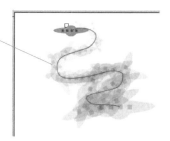

Motion guide orientation

It is possible to alter the way a motion tween moves along the motion guide path. This can have a significant effect, depending on the type of object being tweened.

1 Double-click on the first frame of the linked layer (not the Motion Guide layer). In the Frame Properties dialog box, select the Tweening tab

2 By default the 'Orient to path direction' box is checked on. This means that the centre point of the tweened object is rotated around the guide path

3 Check off the 'Orient to path direction' box to keep the object parallel as it follows the guide path

Shape tweening

Shapes such as ovals and rectangles are excellent for shape tweening into letters or numbers.

The third type of animation that can be performed in Flash is shape tweening, or morphing. This is where one shape changes into another during the course of the animation e.g. turning a letter A into a number 2. This type of animation can only be done with simple shapes, broken apart text and stage level objects. Shape tweening cannot be applied to symbols, groups or bitmaps. To create a shape tween:

Shape tweening is an effective technique but it should not be overused in a movie, or else the impact will be diminished.

1 Select File > New to open a new movie. In frame 1 select the Text tool from the Drawing toolbar and type the letter A in a large font size (72 points or above)

A blank keyframe is inserted in frame 20 because the content is completely different from the previous keyframe. If the content was the same but was going to appear in a different position (as in a motion tween) then a regular keyframe would have been inserted rather than a blank one.

2 Select the A on the Stage and select Modify > Break Apart from the Menu bar. This will turn the text into a format suitable for shape tweening

3 Select frame 20 and insert a blank keyframe (Insert > Blank Keyframe from the Menu bar). With the Text tool, type the number 2, the same size as the A in frame 1. Break it apart as above

If you are using text for motion tweening and the tween does not work properly, make sure that both pieces of text are broken apart.

The Distributive and Angular options in the Tweening dialog box determine how the tween operates. The Distributive option is better for curved objects; Angular is better for objects with straighter lines and corners.

It is possible to tween more than one letter or number together, but the results are erratic. If you want to shape tween a whole word, do it by putting each letter on a separate layer and creating each tween individually.

4 Double-click on frame 1 to access the Frame Properties dialog box. Select the Tweening tab and select Shape as the type of tweening. Select OK

5 Turn on onion skinning to see the path of the shape tween

6 It is possible to change the size, colour and orientation of the tweened objects, in their keyframes, by using the drawing tools and their modifiers. This can give added effect. Here, the 2 has been resized and rotated and this is reflected during the tween

Shape hints

Sometimes the results of a shape tween can be less than ideal; during the course of the tween the object looks more like an ungainly blob rather than one item morphing into another. To improve the tweening process, it is possible to add shape hints to each object. These are corresponding points on each object that act as guides for the tween to follow. To add shape hints to a shape tween:

Up to 26 shape hints can be added to the objects in a shape tween. These are labelled a–z.

Each object in the shape tween has to have the same shape hint applied to it, i.e. if the first object has an 'a' shape hint then the second object has to have the same one.

1 Select the object in frame 1. Select Modify>Transform> Add Shape Hint from the Menu bar

2 Position the shape hint on the object in frame 1

3 Move to the object in frame 20 and position the shape hint in the same corresponding position as for the object in frame 1

When a shape hint is added to the first object, the corresponding shape hint will appear when you select the frame containing the second object. It can then be placed by clicking and dragging it.

4 Continue until a suitable number of shape hints have been added to each object

Animating text

One of the most common uses for Flash on the Web is creating animated text. This is where text moves across the screen from left to right, or vice versa, or fades in and out from a particular point. In some cases, numerous pieces of text are animated within a single movie and, if it is done well, this can create a visually striking effect. To create animated text:

1 Create a text block and convert it into a graphic symbol. Create a motion tween to move it across the screen

Watch me go

2 Double-click the text on the Stage in frame 1 to access the Instance Properties dialog. Select Color Effect>Alpha and enter 0%. This makes the text in frame 1 transparent; it fades in as the tween progresses

3 Create tweens with text on several layers for added effect. Vary the start and end points of the tweens to achieve variety

Watch me go

I fade in
and out

And me too

Movie clips

Movie clips are symbols that act like self contained animations: they have their own timeline and once they are created they are placed in the Library. They can then be reused by inserting them anywhere on the main Timeline. This is useful if you have an animation that you want to use several times. To create a movie clip symbol:

Any elements that can be added to an animation in the main editing environment can also be added to a movie clip symbol.

1 Select Insert>New Symbol from the Menu bar. Name the symbol and select Movie Clip

No matter how long a movie clip symbol is (and they can extend over dozens of frames) they are always placed in one frame on the main Timeline.

2 Movie clip Editing Mode looks the same as the main Editing Mode, except that the movie clip icon is shown here. Create the animation as you would for one on the main Stage

Movie clips can be added to interactive buttons (see Chapter Ten).

3 When the movie clip is completed, click on the scene number to return to the main Editing Mode. The movie clip symbol will be placed in the Library and can be reused throughout the movie

Interactivity

Giving the user the power to interact with a movie is an important part of Flash. This chapter looks at the ways in which this interactivity can be achieved with frames and buttons and also looks at some options for using interactive actions.

Covers

Types of interactivity | 158

Frame actions | 159

Adding Stop and Play actions | 162

Adding Go To actions | 163

Inserting a preloader | 165

Button symbols | 167

Adding actions to buttons | 170

Adding movie clips and sounds | 172

Chapter Ten

Types of interactivity

In addition to its graphical and animated elements, another important aspect of Flash is its interactive functions. These can allow the movie author to instruct the program to perform certain actions when it reaches a certain frame, or an action can be performed when the user clicks on a particular button. Also, interactivity can be achieved with text fields, where an action is performed as a result of the user entering text in an editable text box.

Text fields are one of the more complex types of interactivity. More information can be obtained about them by selecting Help>Flash Help Topics from the Menu bar, then selecting Using Type>Creating text fields and editable text, in the Context Help.

For interactivity to occur in a movie there need to be certain elements present:

- An event, which is something that sets the action in progress. This can be a movie reaching a particular frame or the user clicking a button

- An action, which is performed when the event occurs

- A target, which is the item upon which the action is performed

Actions can be inserted into frames or button symbols. If it is a frame action it can be inserted in the layer where the interactivity is to take place, or it can be placed on a separate layer. In a button symbol the action can be placed in one of the states of the button i.e. when the cursor is moved over it, when it is clicked on or when the mouse button is released.

If an action is inserted on a separate layer, the action will apply to all of the frames at that point in the movie, regardless of how many layers there are.

A frame with an action inserted. This is denoted by the small 'a'

Creating interactivity with actions can be a complex business, using some elements of computer programming, the finer points of which could take a whole book themselves. This chapter gives an overview of interactivity and shows some of the commands that can be used.

Frame actions

Frame actions are placed in a frame and when the Timeline reaches this frame the action passes on an instruction. This could be to stop a movie playing at that point, turn off any sound that is playing or jump to another frame within the movie.

Adding frame actions

1 Double-click on the frame where you want to add the action. The Frame Properties dialog box appears. Click on the Actions tab

2 Click here to access the Actions menu

3 Select an action. This will appear in the Actions dialog box. Any parameters for the selected action appear here

...cont'd

Some frame actions – such as Stop, Play, Toggle High Quality, Stop All Sounds and Go To – are reasonably straightforward. Others – such as FS Command, Set Property and Set Variables – require a certain amount of programming knowledge.

Types of actions

The actions that can be inserted into a frame are:

- *Go To.* This instructs the movie to jump to the specified frame

- *Play.* This instructs a movie to begin playing

- *Stop.* This stops the movie playing at the specified point. It can be restarted using the Play action

- *Toggle High Quality.* This displays graphics at a higher or lower quality. Also referred to as antialiasing

- *Stop All Sounds.* This turns off any sounds that are playing at this point in the movie

- *Get URL.* This instructs the movie to open the specified URL i.e. Web page

- *FS Command.* This lets your movie communicate with the program that is hosting it i.e. a Web browser

For a fuller look at frame actions select Help>Flash Help Topics from the Menu bar and select Creating Interactive Movies.

- *Load/Unload Movie.* This loads, or unloads, a movie into a Web page

- *Tell Target.* This can be used to interact with other Flash movies by using actions within the current one

- *If Frame is Loaded.* This instructs the movie to perform an action if a certain frame has already been downloaded

- *If.* This checks to see if a particular statement is true or false. Depending on the outcome, a specific action is performed

- *Loop.* This keeps performing an action while a certain condition is in place. If the condition is removed then the loop stops

- *Call*. This performs a set of actions

- *Set Property*. This allows you to edit items in a movie as it is playing

- *Set Variable*. This is used to process data that has a variable value, such as text entered into a text box

- *Duplicate/Remove Movie Clip*. This duplicates or removes movie clips as the movie is playing, depending on the action taken by the user

- *Drag Movie Clip*. This allows for movie clips to be draggable objects while the movie is playing

When an action is deleted there is no warning box asking if you are sure you want to delete the action. This may not be a problem if it is a simple action such as a 'Stop' one. However, if it is a more complicated action, with several parameters, it could take longer to regenerate it. Make sure you really want to delete an action before you do so.

- *Trace*. This generates a message when an action is performed. This does not appear in the published movie but it can be useful when testing a movie

- *Comment*. These are individual comments that are placed in an action script to remind yourself of a certain thing or explain what a certain item does. They do not appear in the published movie

Deleting actions

Any action can be deleted from within the Actions dialog box:

2 Click here to delete the action

1 Access the Actions dialog box as described on page 159. Select the action to be deleted

Click here to change the order of the actions by moving them up or down

Adding Stop and Play actions

Two of the most commonly used actions are Stop and Play. These do exactly as they say and they can be used at the beginning of a movie or at any point throughout it. The Stop action halts the whole movie at the point where the action is inserted. To restart the movie a Play action has to be activated after the Stop action. Stop actions can be used to stop an animation playing continuously (see page 146). To add Stop and Play actions:

By default, a Flash movie on the Web plays automatically once it is loaded. If you want to pause it at the start, add a Stop action in frame 1 of the movie. This could be used if you want the movie to begin only after the user has performed an action, such as clicking on a button.

If a movie is being used as a stand-alone application, the default is to pause it. To make it play automatically, a Play action (or a Go To and Play action) would have to be inserted in frame 1.

1 Select the frame where you want the movie to stop

2 Double-click on the frame to open the Frame Properties dialog box

3 Select the Actions tab and select Stop

4 Add any other actions you want to include after the Stop action and add Play to restart the movie

Adding Go To actions

Unless instructed otherwise a movie will play all of its frames sequentially. However, by using actions it is possible to change the order in which the frames are played. This could be used if your movie was an interactive game. In one frame could be a question, and the movie would then move to different frames depending on the answer given. To do this you have to insert values for each Go To action. To insert a Go To action:

The Go To action can be used to great effect when it is inserted into a button. See later in this chapter for information about interactive buttons.

The Go To action can be used to jump to any frame in any scene in the movie.

Labels can be used to identify frames as the destination for Go To action, rather than just the frame number.

1 Select a frame where you want a Go To action and access the Actions dialog box as shown on the facing page. Select Go To

2 The Go To action is added in the Actions dialog box. By default it goes to the first frame of the current scene. This can be changed if required

3 Select a different scene by clicking here and choosing one from the drop-down list

If the target frame for a Go To action is the previous one then there is a danger of inserting an unwanted loop in the movie. If the movie goes back to the previous frame, plays its content and then moves onto the next frame, the Go To action will send it back again, and so on. Another action would have to be inserted in the target frame to avoid it going straight to the next sequential frame (unless a loop effect was intended).

4 Select a target frame for the Go To action by clicking on one of these buttons. This can be a frame number, a label, an expression (a formula based on variable information) or the next or previous frame

5 By default, the Go To action also inserts a Stop action. To enable the movie to play immediately from the target frame check the Go to and Play box on

By default, the Enable Frame Actions option is checked off. This is because it can be irritating for the frame actions to be active when you are editing a movie.

6 Select Control> Enable Frame Actions from the Menu bar to allow you to see how frame actions operate, while you are still in Editing Mode

Inserting a preloader

To rename a scene, select Modify> Scene and type in the scene name in the Scene Properties dialog box.

If you have created a long movie, it may take a few seconds for it to download and start playing. This could lead to the user concluding that, since nothing is happening, they should move on somewhere else. To overcome this problem it is possible to create a preloader. This is a message or small animation that assures the user that the movie is loading and will appear shortly. To create a preloader:

Make sure the preloader scene comes before the main movie one.

1 Create a new movie by selecting File>New from the Menu bar. Create a minimum of two scenes, one for the preloader and one for the main part of the movie. Name Scene 2 Main Movie and create your

movie. Name Scene 1 Preloader and enter suitable content on the Stage

Since Flash movies use streaming, only part of a movie has to be downloaded before it starts playing. Therefore, when specifying a frame that has to be loaded it does not have to be the last one in the movie. It just has to be enough of the movie to allow it to play while the rest is downloading.

2 Insert a new layer and call this Preload Actions. Double-click on frame 1. In the Actions dialog box, select If Frame is Loaded

and specify a frame in the Main Movie scene. This specifies the target frame that has to be loaded before the next action takes effect

...cont'd

The preloader will keep playing until the criteria in the If Frame Is Loaded action are met. If this takes a reasonable amount of time (over 30 seconds) then it is worth creating a preloader scene that can hold the user's attention.

3 Enter a Go To and Play action underneath the If Frame Is Loaded action. This is the action that will be

performed if the criteria for the first action are met i.e. frame 1 of Main Movie will start playing if frame 50 has already been loaded. If it is not met it will move to the next frame

If a movie is short or small in file size, the preloader may be redundant because the target frame for loading will be in place even before the preloader can be displayed.

4 Insert a keyframe in frame 2 of the preloader scene and double-click on it. In the Actions dialog box,

When adding the Go To action, make sure to check on the Go to and Play box, otherwise the movie will stop.

enter a Go To and Play action and set the parameters as current scene, frame 1. This will send the Timeline back to frame 1 of the preloader scene. It will then check the actions here. If the criteria have not been met it will go to frame 2 again and so on. Once the criteria in frame 1 are met the Timeline will go to the Main Movie scene and begin playing at the specified frame

Button symbols

Creating button symbols

As well as inserting actions into frames in a movie, interactive actions can also be used in buttons. These are a type of symbol that react in certain ways when they are clicked by the user or even when the mouse cursor passes over them. Button symbols can be used in the same way as other symbols: they are created in symbol Editing Mode which then places them in the Library. They can then be dragged onto the Stage, where they become instances of the original button symbol. When a button is created it has four elements, or states:

Using different coloured gradient fills for each state of a button symbol can produce a satisfying effect, where the button appears to glow.

- *Up*. This is how the button appears initially on the Stage, before it has been accessed

- *Over*. This is how the button appears when the mouse cursor is passed over it

- *Down*. This is how the button appears when it is clicked on by the user

- *Hit*. This is the area around the button that is active i.e. if it is clicked it activates the appropriate state. The hit state is invisible in the published movie

Button symbols always have four frames and they act like mini movie clips.

To create a button symbol:

1 Select Insert>New Symbol from the Menu bar

Insert	Modify	Control	Libraries	Wi
Convert to Symbol...				F8
New Symbol...				Ctrl+F8

2 In the Symbol Properties dialog name the button and select Button as its behaviour. Click OK

Symbol Properties

Name: Press me

Behavior: ○ Graphic ● Button ○ Movie Clip

OK Cancel Help

It is possible to tell when you are in button symbol Editing Mode because the button symbol and its name are highlighted at the top of the Timeline, next to the scene name. Also, the four frames have the names of the corresponding button states above them i.e. Up, Over, Down and Hit.

3 Symbol Editing Mode for a button symbol is activated. This is automatically created with four frames, with a keyframe pre-inserted in the first one. The crosshair on the Stage denotes the centre of the button. Draw a circle around the crosshair

Insert a blank keyframe by selecting Insert> Blank Keyframe from the Menu bar.

4 Select the Over frame and insert a blank keyframe. Draw a square around the crosshair

If you only want to make small changes to an object in a preceding keyframe, such as changing the colour, use the Insert>Keyframe command.

5 Select the Down frame and insert a blank keyframe. Draw a triangle around the crosshair

You can make the area defined for the Hit state any colour you like, since it does not appear in the published movie. However, it is a good idea to make it a different colour from the first three states of the button. This way you will know what is the Hit state when you are in symbol Editing Mode.

6 Select the Hit frame and insert a blank keyframe. Draw an object around the crosshair that is large enough to cover the biggest object in the button. This is the area that will activate the button

7 Click on the scene name to return to the main Editing Mode. The button symbol will have been placed in the Library. Select the button and click and drag to create an instance on the Stage

If the Library is not visible, select Window> Library from the Menu bar.

If you try to edit a button instance while Enable Buttons is active, you will only see the different states of the button. Deselect this to perform editing tasks on the Stage.

8 Select Control>Enable Buttons from the Menu bar. This enables you to see how the button performs in its different states, without having to leave the main Editing Mode. The button can also be tested by selecting Control>Test Movie (or Test Scene)

Adding actions to buttons

The same actions that are used for frames can also be used for buttons. However, they are triggered in a slightly different way since button actions are activated by the mouse and there are several options available for this. This means that you have to specify which mouse event you want to use to start the action. To add an action to a button:

 Button actions should be added to the instance on the Stage rather than the symbol in the Library.

1 Place an instance of a button symbol on the Stage. Access the Instance Properties dialog box by either double-clicking on the instance or selecting Modify > Instance from the Menu bar

 Button actions can be added to the button without first selecting an On MouseEvent. In this case the default mouse event is added (see the facing page).

2 Select the Actions tab and select On MouseEvent from the Actions menu

3 Select a mouse event that will activate the button action

When an action is added to a button the default mouse event to trigger this action is Release i.e. the action will be triggered when the mouse button is released in the Down state of the button. To change this, deselect the Release mouse event and select another from the list.

The possible mouse event options are:

- *Press*, which occurs when the mouse button is pressed while the cursor is within the Hit area of a button

- *Release*, which occurs when the mouse button is released within the Hit area

- *Release Outside*, which occurs when the mouse button is released when the cursor has been dragged outside the Hit area

- *Roll Over*, which occurs when the mouse cursor moves into the Hit area

- *Roll Out*, which occurs when the mouse cursor is moved out of the Hit area

- *Drag Over*, which occurs when the mouse button is held down and dragged out of the Hit area and then back into it

- *Drag Out*, which occurs when the mouse button is clicked within the Hit area and then dragged outside it

- *Key Press*, which can be used to specify a key on the keyboard to trigger the action

More than one mouse event can be added to a single button.

Using actions and mouse events can create highly sophisticated interactive movies. However, to do this some knowledge of computer programming such as Actionscripting is necessary.

4 Select the relevant mouse event and select the action or actions that will be triggered by this

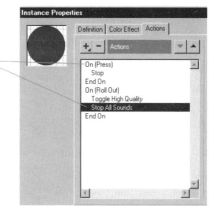

Adding movie clips and sounds

Fully animated buttons can be created by using different movie clips for each state of the button. This means the animation will change in appearance, according to how the user is interacting with the button.

Movie clips

To make buttons more versatile it is possible to add movie clips to them. This means that when the button is pressed (or whatever mouse event that has been assigned to it) a movie clip plays. Movie clips can be inserted in the separate states of a button and different ones can be used within the same button. To add a movie clip to a button:

1 Double-click on a button symbol in the Library to access symbol Editing Mode

If you are using only movie clips to create a button, make sure that the Hit area of the button is big enough to cover the area of the largest movie clip.

2 Select a state of the button (Up, Over or Down) and drag a movie clip over the button centrepoint. The clip will play when this state of the button is activated

To learn more about adding sounds to a movie, select Help>Flash Help Topics from the Menu bar and then select Adding sound from the Context Help.

Sounds

Sound files can be added to buttons in the same way as movie clips: open the button in symbol Editing Mode, select the Up, Over or Down state and drag a sound file from the Library onto the Stage. This can be a useful technique to alert the user to whether they have performed a particular action with the button i.e. one sound for when they press the button and another for when they release it. Different sounds can be added to the first three states of a button.

Testing and publishing

The final part of producing a Flash movie is testing it to ensure it works properly and then publishing it for people to see. This chapter looks at ways to test the elements of a movie, set publishing options and then publish a movie, either on the Web or as a stand-alone application.

Covers

Testing options | 174

Testing environment | 176

Preparing to publish | 180

More publishing options | 184

Publishing a movie | 185

Publishing on the Web | 186

Chapter Eleven

Testing options

The Controller is a quick way to test animations without having to leave the authoring environment. Another way is to drag the Playhead along the Timeline, although this may not play it at a consistent speed.

As with any project that is going to be viewed by a large audience, it is important to test movies thoroughly before they are published. Within a Flash movie there can be a number of complex elements and it is essential to make sure that everything is working properly, both independently and as part of the whole movie. Flash has several testing options and the ones in the authoring environment are:

The Controller

This plays a movie through in the authoring environment. It shows animations but buttons and frame actions are inactive. To use the Controller:

1. Select Window>
   Controller from the
   Menu bar

The Controller can be moved around the screen by clicking the top bar and dragging.

2. Use the controls to
   play the movie:

Rewind   Play   Go to end

Stop   Back one   Forward
frame   one frame

The Enable Frame Actions and Enable Buttons options should only be used when you want to test these items. Otherwise they could interfere with other editing processes.

Enable buttons and frames

Frame actions and buttons can be viewed in the authoring environment:

Select Control>Enable Frame Actions (or Control>Enable Buttons) in the Menu bar

...cont'd

When it is first accessed, the testing environment will look similar to the authoring one. The only difference is that most of the Menu bar and toolbar options are greyed out. However, there are a number of features that can be accessed in the testing environment that allow greater versatility when testing a movie. These are looked at on the following pages.

Rather than just testing individual parts of a movie, as with the options in the authoring environment on the facing page, it is also possible to test an entire scene or movie to see how it will appear when it is published:

Testing scenes

To test an individual scene:

1. Open the scene you want to test and select Control>Test Scene from the Menu bar

2. This will open the selected scene and play it in the testing environment. Animations, frame actions and buttons will all be active

To return to the authoring environment from the testing one, close down the testing window or select File>Close from the Menu bar.

Testing movies

This performs a very similar task to Test Scene, except that it tests all of the scenes in a movie, in the order in which they will play when the movie is published. To test a movie:

Select Control>Test Movie from the Menu bar

Testing environment

When a Flash movie is played over a browser on the Web it is impossible to predict how it will appear on every user's computer. This is because of the wide range of browsers being used, processor speeds and modem speeds: on one computer the movie may play perfectly, but on another it may take longer to download and play erratically. Flash has a number of functions to test how a movie will play in different circumstances.

Test movies at the lowest download speed first (14.4K). If they work well at this speed then there should be no problem at the higher speeds. However, test them at the higher ones too, just to make sure.

Testing download speeds

Due to the diversity of modems used by people when accessing the Internet it is certain that your movie will be downloaded at a variety of speeds. You can test how various options will look by using the streaming option in the testing environment:

The User Settings and the Customize option for download speeds can be used for settings outside the most commonly used ones which are 14K, 28K and 56K. The custom settings can be used for high speed connections or if the movie is being used on an intranet. If this is the case, check the required setting with your system administrator.

1 In the testing environment for a scene or a movie, select Control from the Menu bar and select the required download speed

2 Select Control> Show Streaming to see how your movie will play at the selected download speed

...cont'd

Streaming is a technique which allows a movie to start playing when only part of the whole movie has been downloaded. If this works properly the movie should play smoothly throughout.

However, problems can occur if there are very large frames in a movie since the movie will already be playing and the downloading will be slowed down. If the playback of the movie catches up with the streaming download then there could be a pause in the playing of the movie.

Bandwidth Profiler

A Bandwidth Profiler is available in the testing environment and this can display several items of useful information about the streaming of the movie and how individual frames affect this. To view the Bandwidth Profiler:

1 In the testing environment select View>Bandwidth Profiler from the Menu bar

2 The Bandwidth Profiler is displayed above the movie

The elements of the Bandwidth Profiler are:

- *Dim.* This is the dimensions of your movie, in pixels

- *Fr Rate.* This is the Frames Per Second speed at which your movie is set to play

- *Size.* This is the file size of the entire movie or scene

- *Duration.* This is the total number of frames in the movie (or scene). The number beside it, in brackets, is the time the movie (or scene) will take to play, in seconds

To maximise streaming, try to use symbols frequently in a movie and bitmaps and sounds sparingly.

- *Preload*. This is the time the movie will take to download before it starts to play. This information is particularly relevant if you want to include a preloader with a movie (see Chapter Ten)

- *Bandwidth*. This is the bandwidth speed that has been selected to test the download speed of the movie

- *Frame*. The first number is where the Playhead is currently situated and the one underneath it displays a selected frame's size in relation to the whole movie

- *Loaded*. The first number displays how many frames of the movie have been downloaded and the one underneath displays the amount of the file that has been downloaded

Select Control> Show Streaming to view how the movie will download. A green line moves along the Timeline to indicate how much of the movie has been downloaded in the background. The cursor indicates where the movie's Playhead is currently positioned. If the two meet and stop, this could indicate a problem area in the downloading of a movie.

Streaming Graph

When used in conjunction with the Bandwidth Profiler the Streaming Graph can identify potential problem areas for when a movie is downloading. To access the Streaming Graph:

1 In the testing environment, select View>Streaming Graph

2 Bars above this (red) line indicate frames that could cause a problem when downloading

Frame By Frame graph

Another option for assessing the downloading speed of a movie is the Frame By Frame graph. This shows the size of each frame in a movie. To view the Frame By Frame graph:

If a few frames stand out as being a lot bigger in size than the others in the movie, return to the authoring environment and see if they can be edited.

1 In the testing environment, select View>Frame By Frame Graph

2 The size of each individual frame in the movie is displayed in the graph. Select an individual frame to view its properties in the Bandwidth Profiler

On the View menu, toggle High Quality on and off to see the graphics in the movie at a higher or lower quality.

Preparing to publish

The object of creating any Flash movie is to have it published. This can be onto a CD-ROM as a stand-alone application, but the most common use for Flash movies is to publish them on the Web or an intranet.

The method for publishing Flash movies on the Web is to insert them into an HTML document. If you look at the code for a file on the Web containing a Flash movie you may want to run screaming from your computer, never to think of Flash or HTML again. At first sight it does look confusing, even if you have some experience of producing Web pages. The good news is that you only have to specify a few settings and Flash does all of the complicated work for you. This is done by instructing Flash to create an HTML document with the Flash movie inserted in it. However, before this, certain settings can be chosen to determine the way the movie will look when it is published.

If you select HTML as a format for publishing your movie, the Flash option is selected automatically, if it is not already.

Publish settings for the Web

To determine the settings for a movie on the Web:

Flash can create files in several formats and it is possible to give each file type a different name. However, for the sake of consistency it is better to keep the same root name for all formats (the extension will be different for each type). The default uses the same name for each format.

1 In the authoring environment, select File > Publish Settings

2 Select Flash and HTML as the type. This will create a Flash movie file (Shockwave Flash or .SWF) and an HTML file (.HTM)

If you click on the Info button next to the Template box there will be a description of the template and any HTML tags it uses.

3 In the Publish Settings dialog box select the HTML tab

HTML settings

Within the HTML dialog box there are various settings to determine the appearance of the Flash movie in your HTML document:

The options for specifying the dimensions of a published movie do not affect its positioning within the HTML window, just its location in the movie window.

- *Template.* This is how the movie is inserted into the HTML document. The simplest one is the default, Flash Only, which uses EMBED and OBJECT tags to display the movie depending on which browser it is being viewed on (EMBED for Netscape Navigator or Communicator and OBJECT for Internet Explorer). The other available templates are: Flash with FS Command; Image Map; Java Player; QuickTime; and User Choice. These can be used to give extra functionality to a movie, but if you are not confident with these then the default is more than adequate

- *Dimensions.* This dictates how the movie will appear within a movie window within the HTML document window. The default is to match the size set in the Movie Properties dialog box. However, the size can also be set in pixels or as a percentage to make the movie larger or smaller than the movie window, as appropriate

In order to get the correct position for your published movie, experiment with the Dimensions, Scale and Flash Alignment settings to see how different combinations appear in a browser.

- *Playback*. The options here determine the properties for when the movie is played in a browser. These are: Paused At Start, which means the movie does not start playing until the user performs an action such as clicking a button; Display Menu, which displays a contextual menu about the Flash Player if the user right-clicks (Windows) or Ctrl+clicks (Mac); Loop, which will cause the movie to keep playing after its initial playback; and Device Font (Windows only), which substitutes suitable fonts if the ones in the movie are not installed on the user's computer

- *Quality*. This can be used to get the best balance between playback speed and image quality. The options range from Low, which is the fastest speed and the lowest image quality, to Best, which offers the top image quality but the slowest playback speed

- *HTML Alignment*. This can be used if you create an HTML page with other items in addition to the Flash movie. This allows you to align the movie with the other items on the page. The options are Left, Right, Top and Bottom

HTML editors can be used to include additional content, as well as the Flash movie.

- *Scale*. If you have changed the dimensions of the movie from its original settings this can be used to determine how it is scaled within the movie window. The options are: Show All, which scales the movie proportionately to fit the movie window; No Border, which will display the movie at its actual size even if it is bigger than the movie window; and Exact Fit, which scales the movie to fit exactly into the whole movie window

- *Flash Alignment*. This can be used to determine the movie's position within the movie window. The options are for Horizontal – Left, Center and Right; and for Vertical – Top, Center and Bottom

- *Show Warning Messages*. This alerts the user to any problems with the HTML coding

...cont'd

The Flash settings apply to whatever format the movie is published in, not just HTML.

Flash settings

In addition to determining the HTML settings for a movie, the same can be done for Flash settings.

Select the Flash tab in the Publish Settings dialog box

The Flash settings are:

- *Load Order.* This lets you set the order in which layers within a frame are loaded into the browser. The options are for Bottom Up or Top Down

- *Generate size report.* If this is checked on, a text file will be created with a report on the size of each frame in the movie

When setting the JPEG quality, a setting of '0' will create images with the lowest quality and '100' the highest.

- *Protect from import.* This stops anyone copying your movie and using it as their own

- *Omit Trace actions.* This stops anyone being able to look at the code that makes up a movie

- *JPEG Quality.* This can be used to set the quality of JPEG images

Stream sounds are those that download while the movie is playing; event sounds are those that are played when a specific action occurs, such as a button being pressed.

- *Audio Stream.* This can be used to compress streamed sounds

- *Audio Event.* This can be used to compress event sounds

- *Version.* This can be used so earlier version of the Flash Player can view your movie

More publishing options

Although HTML is the most common way to publish Flash movies there are a number of other options, which can all be accessed by selecting the Formats tab in the Publish Settings dialog box. The other formats are:

- *Projectors*. These are stand-alone applications that act like mini programs, that can be played on almost any computer. Everything that is needed to play the movie is contained within the projector file and it is just a case of opening it from a CD-ROM, a floppy disk or a hard drive

- *QuickTime*. This is a video and multimedia file format that has been developed by Apple and it is widely used for playing videos on the Web. The QuickTime format has its own dialog box and a Flash movie can be incorporated with other items in a QuickTime movie. The QuickTime dialog box lets you set the size of the QuickTime movie and how the Flash movie interacts with other elements

- *Graphic formats.* There are dialog boxes for three different graphic formats: GIFs, JPEGs and PNGs. This allows you to apply a variety of settings to determine how these images are displayed in the published movie

Projectors are an excellent way to distribute Flash movies, particularly as the user does not require a Flash Player or any other plug-in to play them.

To download the QuickTime 4 plug-in visit the following Web site:

• *http://www.apple.com/*

All file formats for a Flash movie (except Projector) have their own dialog boxes. Click a tab in the Publish Settings dialog to access them

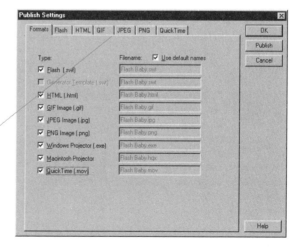

Publishing a movie

Once you have chosen the format, or formats, for your movie and assigned the necessary settings it is time to publish your work.

Previewing

It is possible to publish a movie into several different formats. Select each format in the Publish Settings dialog. When you select Publish, Flash will create the appropriate files for all of these formats.

Before the movie is actually published it is possible to see exactly what it will look like in each of the chosen formats:

Select File>Publish Preview from the Menu bar and select the format in which you want to view the movie

The Projector format creates the largest file size of all Flash formats.

Publishing

If you are satisfied with the preview of your movie you can then publish it:

Select File>Publish from the Menu bar

Movie file (.SWF)   Authoring file (.FLA)

After step 1, Flash creates files for all of the formats that were selected in the Publish Settings dialog and places them in the same folder as the original movie.

Projector file   HTML file

Publishing on the Web

An HTML file is made up of a set of instructions that tell the browser what to display at certain points. Since the Flash movie is referred to in the HTML document it has to be on the server too so that the browser can display it.

If you are publishing a Flash movie on the Web you will need to upload your HTML file and the Flash movie file (.SWF) to the Web server where your site will be hosted. Check with you Internet Service Provider (ISP), or system administrator if you are publishing over an intranet, that they are capable of displaying Flash and ask if there are any specific settings they require.

Once your HTML page is published the source code will look something like this:

Of the two files that are created when a movie is put together, the movie itself has a .SWF extension and the authoring file has a .FLA extension.

(The .SWF file is the one that is uploaded to the Web server.)

This HTML coding is generated by Flash during the Publish process

Using an HTML editor

Flash movies can make up the entire contents of an HTML document. However, if you use an HTML editor (such as Microsoft FrontPage, Adobe Go Live, Adobe PageMill or Macromedia DreamWeaver), it is possible to create additional content on the HTML page. This is an excellent way to combine a Flash movie into a larger HTML document on the Web. There are two important considerations when you are publishing Flash sites on the Web:

If you are including a link on a Web page for downloading the Flash Player, it should go to:

• http://www.macromedia. com/shockwave/ download/

(Omit all spaces in the address.)

- Always include a plain HTML version of your site, for users who do not have the Flash Player installed, or who do not want to download it

- Include a link for those users who want to download the latest version of the Flash Player

Index

Actions   33
   Button   158
   Deleting   161
   Frame   158
      Adding   159
   Go To   163
   On MouseEvent   170
   Stop   146
   Stop and Play   162
   Types   160
Actions menu   159
Adobe
   Go Live   186
   Illustrator   110
   PageMill   12, 186
   Photoshop   112
AIFF files   117
Animation   12
   Animating text   155
   Frame By Frame   12, 138, 144
   Guided   12
   Motion guides   150
      Orientation   151
   Motion tweening   138, 147
      Editing   149
   Shape tweening   138, 152
      Shape hints   154
   Tweening   12
Antialiasing   160
Apple   184
Arrow tool. *See* Drawing toolbar

Background colour   25
Bandwidth   8, 177–178
Bandwidth Profiler
   Dim   177
   Duration   177

Fr Rate   177
Frame   178
Loaded   178
Preload   178
Size   177
Bitmaps   9, 88, 95, 110
   As fills   114
   Converting items into   110
   Editing fills   115
   Importing   111
   Properties   112
   Tracing   113
   Types   110
BMPs   110
Browsers   15
Brush tool. *See* Drawing toolbar
Button symbols
   Creating   167
   Down   167
   Hit   167
   Over   167
   Up   167
Buttons   13. *See also* Symbols: Buttons
   Actions   13
   Adding actions   170
   Adding movie clips   172
   Adding sound   172

Circles
   Drawing   44
Clip art   117
Colour focus   87
Colour palette   80
Colours
   Alpha settings   149
   Gradient   80
      Linear   80

Radial   80
Gradients
  Adding   83
  Selecting   88
Solid   80
  Creating   81
Compression   10
Controller   174
Copy   74
Corner points   61
  Adding   73
Creating a background   124
Curve points   61, 72
Cut   74
Cut-aways. *See* Objects: Creating cut-aways

Digital cameras   111
Dots Per Inch   112
Dpi. *See* Dots Per Inch
Drawing toolbar   42
  Arrow tool   57
    Selecting with   60
  Brush tool   50, 85
  Dropper tool   53
  Eraser tool   54
    Modes   55
  Hand tool   56
  Ink Bottle tool   51
  Lasso tool   58
  Line tool   43
  Magnifier tool   56
  Modifiers   42
  Oval tool   44
  Pencil tool   47
  Rectangle tool   46
DreamWeaver. *See* Macromedia
Dropper tool. *See* Drawing toolbar

EMBED tag   181
Enable Buttons command   169, 174
Enable Frame Actions command   164, 174
Eraser tool. *See* Drawing toolbar

File extensions   18, 20
File size   131
Files
  Opening   20
  Closing   20
Fills   40
  Reshaping   73
Flash   8
  Authoring files   18
  Components   17
  Downloading   14
  Editor   20
  Home page   14
  Installing   16
  Movies   10
    Projectors   11
  Trial version   14
  Windows   21
Flash Player   11
  Downloading   15
  Link for downloading   186
Frame By Frame graph   179
Frame rate   24, 123
Frame By Frame animation. *See* Animation:
    Frame By Frame
Frames   18, 23, 122
  Adding   125
  Comments   128
  Copying   127
  Deleting   127
  Labels   128
  Moving   127
  Properties   128, 159
  Regular   124
Freehand. *See* Macromedia
FrontPage. *See* Microsoft

Generator   34
GIFs   9, 110, 184
Go Live. *See* Adobe
Gradient fills
    Editing   85
Gradients. *See* Colours: Gradients: Adding
Graphical Interchange Format. *See* GIFs
Grid   145

Hand tool. *See* Drawing toolbar
Help Topics   160
Hexadecimal values   82
HTML   11, 18, 180

Illustrator. *See* Adobe
Ink Bottle tool. *See* Drawing toolbar
Inspectors
    Frame   33
    Generator   34
    Object   33
    Scene   34
    Transform   34
Instances   10, 34, 94
    Colour properties   108
    Editing   107
    Interactivity   13
    Types   158
Internet   176
Internet Explorer   181
Internet Service Provider. *See* ISPs
ISPs   186

Java   16
Joint Photographic Experts Group *See* JPEGs
JPEGs   9, 110, 112, 183–184

Keyframes   122, 147, 159
    Adding   126
    Blank   168
    For a visual change   126

Lasso tool   88, 114. *See also* Drawing toolbar
    Selecting with   63
Layer properties   134
Layers   119, 129, 138
    Copying   132
    Current mode   133
    Deleting   132
    Hidden mode   133
    Inserting   131
    Locked mode   133
    Locking   129
    Mask   135
    Outline mode   133
    Stacking order   129
        Changing   130
Library   23, 32, 94–96, 118
    Accessing   96
    Creating new folders   97
    Deleting items   97
    Menu   98
    Opening other libraries   99
Line segments   61
Line tool. *See* Drawing toolbar
Lines
    Editing   64
    Reshaping a curved line   73
    Reshaping straight lines   72
    Selecting   61
    Smoothing   48, 64
    Straightening   48, 64
Looping   164

Macromedia   14, 16, 155, 186
  DreamWeaver   186
  Freehand   110
Magic Wand   88, 114
Magnifier tool.   *See* Drawing toolbar
Mask layers.   *See* Layers: Mask
Menus
  Control   31
  Edit   30
  File   30
  Help   32
  Insert   31
  Libraries   32
  Modify   31
  View   30, 35
  Window   32
Microsoft
  FrontPage   12, 186
  PowerPoint   12
Modems   176
Modifiers.   *See* Drawing toolbar
Morphing.   *See also* Animation: Shape
    tweening
Mouse events
  Drag Out   171
  Drag Over   171
  Key Press   171
  Press   171
  Release   171
  Release Outside   171
  Roll Out   171
  Roll Over   171
Movie clips   156. *See also* Symbols: Movie
    clips
Movie Properties   24
Movies
  Files   18
Multimedia   8

Netscape Navigator   181

OBJECT tag   181
Objects
  Aligning   75
    Match Width and Height   76
  Breaking apart   65
  Creating cut-aways   78
  Grouping   65
  Moving
    Manually   66
    With Inspector   66
  Overlay level   38, 107
  Reshaping   72
  Resizing
    Manually   67
    With dialog box   68
    With Inspector   68
  Rotating   71
    Manually   69
    With dialog box   69
  Selecting   41, 60
  Skewing
    With Inspector   70
  Stacking order   77
  Stage level   38
On MouseEvent.   *See* Actions: On
    MouseEvent
Onion skinning   140, 148
Oval tool.   *See* Drawing toolbar
Overlay level objects   38, 107

PageMill.   *See* Adobe
Paragraph properties   91
Paste   74
Paste in Place   74
Pencil tool.   *See* Drawing toolbar

PICTs 110
Playhead 123, 140
PNGs 9, 110, 184
Portable Network Group. *See* PNGs
PowerPoint. *See* Microsoft
Preferences 36
Preloader 165
Presentations 11
Projectors 184
Publish settings 180, 185
Publishing
  File formats 185
    Dialog boxes 184
  Flash settings
    Audio Event 183
    Audio Stream 183
    Generate Size Report 183
    JPEG Quality 183
    Omit Trace actions 183
    Version 183
  HTML
    Editors 186
    Settings 181
    Dimensions 181
    Flash Alignment 182
    HTML Alignment 182
    Plain version 186
    Playback 182
    Quality 182
    Scale 182
    Show Warning Messages 182
    Templates 181
  Preparation 180
  Previewing 185
  Templates 181

QuickTime 11, 184

Rectangle tool. *See* Drawing toolbar
Resolution 10, 112
RGB colour model 81
Rulers 27, 66

Scale and Rotate 68
Scanner 111
Scenes 104
  Adding 142
  Naming 165
  Renaming 143
Selecting
  Lines 61
  Objects 41, 60
  Freehand selection 63
  Multiple objects 36
  Partial 62
  Polygon selection 63
Setting movie length 124
Shape hints. *See* Animation: Shape tweening
Shape recognition 49
  Assistance 49
Shift-Select 36
Show Streaming command 178
Snap Modifier 57
Sound 117
  Creating 117
  Editing 119
  Event driven 117
  Fading 120
  Importing 118
  Streamed 117
Sound collections 117
Sound Frame properties 120
Sound Recorder 117
Sounds 95
SoundSimple 117
Stage 23, 94
  Colour 25
  Grid 26
Stage level objects. *See* Objects: Stage level

Stand-alone application   162
Streaming   10, 165, 177
Streaming Graph   178
Symbol Editing Mode   104, 168
Symbol Properties dialog box   106, 167
Symbols   10, 34, 94
  Behaviours   95
  Buttons   95, 103
  Duplicating   106
  Edit in Place   105
  Editing   105
  Graphics   95
  Movie clips   95, 103, 156
  New   102

Test Movie command   146, 175
Test Scene command   146, 175
Testing
  Authoring environment   174
  Download speeds
    Custom settings   176
  Testing environment   174, 176
Text
  Adding   89
  Aligning   91
  Animating   155
  Boxes   90
  Breaking apart   92
  Formatting   91
  Label   90
  Modifiers   89
  Reshaping   92
  Resizing   92
  Rotating   92
Text modifiers   89
Text tool   89
Timeline   22, 123, 139
Toggle High Quality command   179
Toolbars   28
  Docking   29
  Mac toolbars   28

  Moving   29
  Windows toolbars   28
    Moving   29
Tooltips   29
Tweening. *See* Animation: Tweening

Undo command   132
URLs
  Going to   160

Vector-based graphics   9, 42
Viewing options   56

Web authoring   11
Web Safe palette   82
Work Area   23, 144
World Wide Web   8